WHAT OTHERS ARE SAYING ABOUT *SMARTER BACKPACKING*

"Jorgen Johansson has a no-nonsense, non-preachy approach, based on his 40 years of wilderness ramblings, designed to help average backpackers shave weight, not comfort or safety, from their loads."
—*Kristin Hostetter, gear editor, Backpacker Magazine.*

"Some authors have a guru approach that's too specific to their personal hiking style, while others fail in offering practical advice because they're too generic and theoretical. SMARTER BACK-PACKING achieves a happy-medium: Jorgen Johansson shares his personal preferences and opinions, but he knows that backpacking is not a 'one size fits all-activity' so he is sure to qualify his views and to recognize the views of others." — *Andrew Skurka, renowned long-distance adventurer and a National Geographic 'Adventurer of the Year' and Backpacker 'Person of the Year'.*

"Most lightweight backpacking books are American and the techniques and equipment described do not always work that well in the wild weather of Northern Europe. This book contains useful advice and techniques for going lightweight in places like Scandinavia and Scotland. Any backpacker wanting to lighten their load could learn much from this book." — *Chris Townsend, outdoor writer and long distance hiker, gear editor of TGO Magazine and author of The Backpacker's Handbook.*

"Jorgen Johansson distils the complexity of wilderness travel into its simplest core concepts, allowing us to enjoy the freedom of backpacking rather than be encumbered by it. His approach is not only a simpler one, but a vastly smarter one." — *Ryan Jordan, Founder, BackpackingLight.com.*

"*SMARTER BACKPACKING* aims t⌐ of ultralight hiking techniques, ra hikers. The spot-on advice is conversational style, rather than around a campfire with Jorgen *Founder and Chairman, Gossamer*

GW00568904

"If you finish a walk with tired limbs, sore back or blistered feet, then this book is for you. Each stage of the journey is covered beautifully, and as you finish each chapter, question your choices and resulting experience. Step away from the marketing hype, the heavy tough stuff does have its place, but is it in your pack?" — *Bob Cartwright, evangelist at www.backpackinglight.co.uk and award winning podcaster at www.theoutdoorsstation.co.uk.*

"I started hiking the Appalachian Trail in a pretty traditional way and came home being a different hiker. My pack would never be that heavy again. I learned a lot about ultralite hiking from 68 year-old hikers Billy Goat and Nimblewill Nomad. Ultralite hiking is not something cool for hardcore hiking kids. It's just making life easier for everybody. For people interested in changing from a heavier to a lighter pack this book is definitely a good starting point." — *Carsten Jost, German long distance hiker, aspiring for The Triple Crown (Appalachian Trail, Pacific Crest Trail done... Continental Divide Trail brewing).*

"*SMARTER BACKPACKING* is an accessible source of theory and technique for lightening your pack. Jorgen Johansson is an experienced lightweight backpacker whose calm and practical presence comes through in his writing. I heartily recommend *SMARTER BACKPACKING* for experienced lightweight backpackers and newbies alike." — *Carol Crooker, former editor-in-chief of Backpacking Light magazine.*

"With a few rules of thumb, Jorgen Johansson puts the finger on the few parts of the equipment that matter, the simplicity of hiking, and the freedom of making the experience of the wild outdoors as lightweight as possible." — *Glenn Mattsing, editor-in-chief, Outside Magazine, Sweden.*

"I've had the pleasure of hiking with Jorgen Johansson, and the book nicely reflects his own personality—innovative and thought provoking, without taking itself too seriously. Read it. You'll be a smarter backpacker when you're done." — *Don Wilson, former gear editor, Backpackinglight.com.*

"This guide simply delivers what it promises, a straightforward guide to lighter and safer backpacking. You could spend hours and hours searching out this advice and guidance on the net. Or you could save a lot of time by acquiring this book. No-nonsense advice and guidance. No messing!" — *Andy Howell, experienced UK hill walker who has made the move into lightweight backpacking, described in his blog Must Be This Way.*

"Jorgen Johansson approaches each piece of gear from the perspective of a heavyweight packer gone lightweight. SMARTER BACKPACKING is basically like having your own personal expert giving you gear advice in a straightforward, honest way. I learned a ton from this book. The more miles I get under my belt, the more I find myself agreeing with him." — *Briand Doble, ultra light and sometimes super ultra light long distance hiker (Triple Crowner, AT yo-yoer and lots more).*

Smarter Backpacking

Smarter Backpacking

or

How every backpacker can apply lightweight
trekking and ultralight hiking techniques

Jorgen Johansson

NUI Publishing
Sweden

This book is a revised translation of the Swedish
original *Lättare packning från A till Ö.*

All photos by the author.

Cover design by Martin Nordesjö

Copyright 2010 by Jorgen Johansson

ISBN 978-91-979055-0-3

Contents

Cornerstones

For photos and updates, see
the live part of this book at
www.smarterbackpacking.com

Personally, I have a tendency to skip chapters called *Foreword* or something similar, so I have chosen another heading, because this is really a necessary chapter for you to read in order to fully assimilate the meaning of the book. Cornerstones are a truthful description.

To start out, this book tells you how to lighten your load in a simple and safe way for 3-season backpacking. With 3-seasons I mean all the time from early summer when the snow is receding, to late fall when it is reclaiming its grip on the wilderness.

You can use the same way of thinking and planning for winter outings. I have experienced that I do very well in winter with lighter gear, better than I would have believed some years ago. But winter, with snow and cold, makes special demands on the hiker; the margins of safety are narrower and the risk of putting your life in danger is greater. For these reasons you cannot use all the tips in this book for winter backpacking.

Also to be noted is that this book is grounded in backpacking in temperate, or even cool, climates, with plenty of moisture and sometimes high winds, i.e. the

Scandinavian tundra mountains, so close to my heart. However, this is a country that puts high demands on equipment, so if you live and hike in less cool and damp parts of the world, perhaps with more foliage to protect your camps from high winds and rain, you can get along with lighter gear.

Much of my inspiration comes from American thru-hikers and ultra light backpackers. I have also hiked in these lands, at times together with some of the leading proponents of lightweight backpacking. All that I have learned helped me develop a technique over more than five years, that I want to share – a backpacking technique that is definitely not super ultra light and maybe not even ultra light, but a technique that will give ordinary hikers, both young and old, a safe and oh so much more comfortable time in the wilds.

The main difference between hiking in, say, the continental United States and Scandinavia is higher demands on shelter in Scandinavia (usually a tent) due to the fact that you are almost always above timberline, without any trees in reach when the wind howls and the rain is driving mostly horizontally. It is in fact comparable to northern Alaska. This type of weather, with low temperatures, abundant precipitation and frequent high winds also puts higher demands on clothes to keep you dry. Rain gear covering you from head to toe is heavier than the more extreme types of super ultra light gear. In warmer climates a hiker sometimes can walk in the rain without rain gear and can keep warm by moving vigorously.

I find many backpacking books to be written in a seemingly objective mode, where it is more or less implied that what the author advocates has come down on tablets of stone from above and are irrevocable truths. Now, like with any book, they do of course contain the authors, hopefully well-founded, but still personal opinions on the subject. So another cornerstone to keep in mind is that this is an outspokenly subjective book. What you will read about here are my personal experiences, my own interpretations of facts, and my opinions. Whether this makes the book more or less reliable or convincing is for you to decide by *your* personal experiences, *your* interpretations of facts and *your* opinions.

In 2007 my first book, *Vandra Fjäderlätt* ("Hike Featherlight"), was published in Swedish. Many readers have told me and others about how their backpacking life changed after reading that book and choosing to go lighter. People reduced 5-10 kilos (11-22 lbs) or more from their packs. A revolution is taking place among the world's backpackers and it will grow even stronger as more people realize how easy it is to lower their pack weight. In 20 years, there will be large numbers of hikers that have never tried anything but light packing.

My first book contained a lot of theory and background to help the readers make their own, well grounded decisions regarding gear, based on the main functions of different pieces of equipment. I made an attempt to counter gear decisions based on conservatism and on sales blurbs. The book you are reading now is more of an easy-to-use handbook. Everything you need to know about a particular piece of gear is found in one chapter. The chapters are placed in alphabetical order. Some basic chapters, like this one, are found in the beginning of the book. Also, the chapters are simply my pack list for overnight hikes. You might find things there that you do not bring, but it is likelier that your own pack list contains more stuff. Be assured that it need not.

Absolutely crucial is the concept of 3 for 3, which has its own chapter. If you use 343, you will find it an easy way to take a quantum leap to a lower pack weight. This is achieved simply by concentrating on the heaviest objects and then work your way down the ladder. If you have a heavy sleeping bag, it is meaningless to save a few grams off your tooth brush.

The only way to a lighter pack is awareness – building awareness that a lighter pack, than many hikers believe is possible, is indeed attainable, as well as an awareness of what different pieces of gear really weigh. The scale is an essential tool, even though you are not taking it along in your pack. Success in most areas, if not all, is based on good planning and paying attention to details. The same is true for the development of a lighter pack. If you do not accept that you need a scale, as well as a willingness to confront some ingrained beliefs, you will find it very difficult to lower your pack weight. At the end of the day, each person's own choices determine the outcome, and the sum of your individual choices is the total weight of the pack. Heavy pack, heavy strides – light pack, light strides.

It may seem obvious that you can benefit most from lowering the weight of the heaviest objects, but I know from my own journey how long it took before I opened my eyes. It is easy to spend a lot of time discussing which spoon is lighter and forget about the weight of your tent, pack or sleep system. For this reason the 343 rule of thumb is paramount. Hence, a separate chapter in this book addresses these "three big ones" in order to show how much there is to gain by getting their combined weight below 3 kilos (6.5 lbs). This is a most critical chapter to read and never ever forget.

To further communicate the weight of the weight, and particularly the weight of the heavy gear, there are some extra clues and pointers below the chapter headings. These show if you can save kilos or grams by choosing lighter or heavier solutions. This indicates which chapters and what gear you should concentrate on. Start with chasing the kilos (pounds) before you go after the grams (ounces).

Among all the gear and technical stuff filling the pages of a book like this it is crucial to remember that gear is a prerequisite, not a goal in itself. The gear is necessary in order for you to take off down the trail and find out what waits behind the next bend; or up across the mountain to find what is beyond the ridge. After a while one begins to wonder if the hike is actually a way of following a trail on the inside of oneself, in order to find out what waits behind the next ridge. Or bend.

To me, hiking is a way to see both how large and small I am as a human being. Many trivialities that have been bouncing around in my mind are peeled away as my legs carry me across the windswept mountains and down into the lush valleys. Walking is the speed we were created to use when travelling through life. In a world where the pace constantly increases, and where the human casualties of this pace also seem to be on the increase, walking has become a balm for both my body and my soul.

It seems more natural to me to seek succour from a fast-paced life style by lowering my pace, instead of seeking out even more adrenaline-triggering activities. I have learned that I cannot escape myself by running. But when I lower my pace, inner peace is much more attainable. On the other hand, you cannot rush inner peace any more than you can hurry love.

My capacity to assimilate the sights of the natural features surrounding me increases, and so does my capacity to discover my own thoughts and follow them to road's end, as the weight of my pack diminishes. My wish for other people to enjoy similar experiences is a driving force behind my writings.

Another driving force is to inspire more people to walk in nature's wonderland, wherever it may be; and to help them not feel afraid of nature that has not been treated by man. As humans, it is not easy for us to feel and act in favour of wildlife we are not aware of. The reasonably untouched, but always threatened, enclaves of nature and wildlife that are still found on our planet do need advocates. David Attenborough, the man behind so many marvellous films about the natural world has said about his work: "I want to show that nature exists – and that it is fragile."

These days, particularly in these days, many more people need to become aware of nature around us. We need to feel nature's presence. Deep in our bones. I think it becomes easier to choose between developing nature's resources and conserving them, if we have experienced that having fewer items in our pack is more of a prerequisite than a barrier for happiness.

343

For photos and updates, see
the live part of this book at
www.smarterbackpacking.com

*Three for three means that the three big ones, pack,
shelter and sleeping system, should not weigh more
than three kilos (6.5 lbs). 343 means not straining
out the gnats before you have dealt with the camels
in your pack. When you have reduced the weight of
the heaviest equipment, you can move on to sorting
out the lighter gear, and in the end you can consider
drilling holes in your toothbrush handles.*

3 for 3 is no absolute for lightening the pack, but it is a
useful goal for being able to take the quantum leap. The
quantum leap could be lowering your pack weight from
20 kilos (45 lbs) to 10 kilos (22 lbs) or from 15 kilos (35
lbs) to 5 kilos (11 lbs). Limiting the weight of the three
big ones is not putting any extreme demands on the gear.
Anyone that wants to do it can achieve it.

If you look at the three big ones as one entity, as
communicating vessels, you create room for
compromises. The separate pieces of gear do not have to
be the lightest imaginable, they just have to weigh less

than three kilos (6.5 lbs) together. You can keep your sturdy tent or your synthetic sleeping bag if you absolutely want to, but then you have to be stricter when it comes to the others of the big three.

On a 500 kilometer hike through Swedish mountains, mostly above timberline, my three big ones where: Pack, 600 grams (1 lb 5 oz), sleeping bag, 685 grams (1 lb 7 oz), two sleeping pads (closed cell + inflatable), 550 grams (1 lb 3 oz) and tent, 490 grams (1 lb 1 oz). The total weight for the three big ones came to about 2,300 grams (5 lbs 2 oz). I used my walking poles as tent poles. They were not included in the calculation, but even if they were, the weight would not amount to three kilos. And this is a demanding country to hike, with no protection from the wind, frequent rains and fairly low temperatures even in summertime.

Some people use lighter gear than I did, but obviously you can also use heavier gear and still pass the 343 test. So, being able to fit the three big ones below three kilos (6.5 lbs) is not something for extreme ultra lighters. Anyone can do it. The main obstacles are lodged in your brain.

When I hike in forested areas with drier and warmer climate than the Scandinavian tundra, I can use a lighter shelter and lighter sleeping gear and manage 243. But that is not really the issue. The issue is bringing down the weight of the three big ones from maybe 8 kilos (19 lbs), which is not an uncommon weight for these. And if you end up with a weight of 3,1 or 3,2 kilos (5 lbs 11 oz or 5 lbs 14 oz) you have still taken a quantum leap in pack weight.

This book is centered around 343, helping the reader to concentrate on minimizing the weight of the heaviest gear. Do not bother with the small fry until you've taken control of the big fry!

"You blind guides! You strain out a gnat but swallow a camel." (*Matthew 23:24*)

Ankle support

For photos and updates, see
the live part of this book at
www.smarterbackpacking.com

*For those of you who have weak ankles there are
special braces that can be used with light shoes. This
makes it possible to use running shoes and save lots
of weight compared to when using traditional
hiking boots.*

Ankle support is a common argument for buying stiff
boots of varying heights – boots that often are very heavy.
Unfortunately, high boots do not automatically give any
great deal of ankle support. In order to support the ankle
they have to be really stiff and tight-fitting, like a pair of
boots for downhill skiing. These do give a very good
ankle support, but they are not very suitable for walking.

In comparison, most hiking boots are much softer
and less tight-fitting around your ankles. But this also
means that they are not as supportive and, in my view,
most of the advantage is gone. High boots are really
more useful as protection from water and abrasion from
rocks and twigs.

So, what we have is high boots that weigh quite a bit

but do not support the ankles as much as we would like to believe. More important for the support is the heel cup and how it is shaped. The heel cup decides how well we "balance" on the sole and heel of the shoe, and how easy or difficult it is for the foot to twist out of position, which is the action that stresses our ankles.

Thus, the good news is that the height of the boots generally does not determine how supportive they are. Trail running shoes used by cross country runners are often excellent for hikers as well.

Cross country runners often strain and sprain their ankles. This is not so much because they use shoes instead of boots, but because they move with much higher speeds than hikers, through rough terrain. Hence, old and worn cross country ankles tend to need better support, from a medical perspective, than the relatively unharmed ankles that we hikers trot around on. That is why different types of ankle braces have been developed for runners, designed to fit into their running shoes.

So, if you have weak ankles, or are just worried that changing from boots to lighter footwear means risking your ankles, these types of braces offer a good solution. There are various constructions, from fairly soft but reinforced paddings that are tightened with hook-and-loop fasteners, to big plastic contraptions with hinges that brings to mind robots in Starwars movies.

Even the heavier and sturdier ankle braces seldom weigh more than 100-200 grams (3-7 oz). Thus, when you combine them with light trail runners you usually do not even come close to carrying the weight of most hiking boots. I find this an excellent solution for experienced as well as inexperienced hikers. You can leave your heavy boots at home and still feel confident about your ankle support.

Backpack

For photos and updates, see the live part of this book at **www.smarterbackpacking.com**

If you have a light load you will do fine with a light backpack. This really contributes to a low base weight as the pack very often is the heaviest piece of gear you carry. The development of light packs means that you do not need a pack heavier than 1,800 grams (4 lbs) to carry 25 kilos (55 lbs). In my experience you also do not need packs with more capacity than 60 litres (3,600 cu inches) for hikes of 7-14 days if you choose your gear according to this book.

The pack belongs to the three big items and is for many hikers the heaviest piece of gear we lug around. Here you can shave off pounds without losing either comfort or safety. Today, many packs on the market are exceedingly heavy and over-engineered with features that very few hikers need, but still are forced to carry every step of the way.

This, however, is changing, although not as rapidly as one would think. Luckily, today lots of light and yet sturdy packs can be found in many stores.

If you do not regularly go tenting in winter conditions, when the gear tends to get bulkier, you do not need to choose an extra roomy pack. The pack I use holds around 50 litres (3,000 cu inches) which is enough for a one week hike, sleeping out and carrying all the food. The pack is also large enough for 3-4 days of winter camping and more than enough for any hike where you spend the nights in cabins.

You may think I offer this advice because I am an extreme ultra-lighter, but that is not the case. If you follow the moderate advice in this book you will end up with a pack base weight of around 6 kilos (13 lbs) excluding food and fuel. So, my advice is that you do not buy a pack bigger than 60 litres (3,600 cu inches), unless you have considerable amounts of extra gear such as cameras, fishing equipment or climbing gear.

If you carry a light load and do your packing with a bit of care you can do without a frame, internal or external, on your pack. A frameless pack of 50-60 litres (3,000-3,500 cu inches) does not need to weigh more than 450-900 grams (1-2 lbs). Frameless packs in this league are usually intended to handle loads up to around 13-15 kilos (30-34 lbs) and these recommendations often have good margins. I have had no problems carrying heavier loads than recommended in several frameless packs. Usually, the extra pounds are food and fuel at the beginning of a hike and therefore up to a kilo (2 lbs) will disappear into your "front pack" (tummy) every day.

If you choose a pack with some kind of frame or support, there is a considerable number of products that weigh between 1-1.8 kilos (2-4 lbs). In my opinion, you do not need to choose a heavier pack unless you regularly plan to carry heavier burdens than 25 kilos (55 lbs) for many days.

A bonus, if you choose a light pack like the ones described, is that they usually are much less expensive than the flagship packs of the large manufacturers. Mostly you will save about 1 Euro/1USD for every 10 grams (1/3 oz) of pack. That is, a pack that weighs 1,000 grams (35 oz) usually costs around 200 Euros/USD less than a pack that weighs 3,000 grams (100 oz). This rule of thumb actually works for most gear, except high-quality down sleeping bags. Of course this might change over time as currencies fluctuate, but is true in 2010, when USD and Euros are worth roughly the same.

If you hike from cabin to cabin and if you can buy some of your food in these cabins, you will virtually never have to carry more than 5,000-6,000 grams (11-13 lbs). Then you can use extremely light packs. Some have a capacity of 30 liters (1,800 cu inches) and only weigh 100-150 grams (3-5 oz). However, the weight penalty is small if you want to choose a slightly sturdier pack. But, for cabin hikes I would not buy a pack that weighs more than 500 grams (1 lb 2oz).

Packing a frameless pack well means that you should try to create a frame with the gear you put in the pack. Things that are long and stiff go closer to your back, in order to keep the pack from collapsing like an accordion.

Tent poles are good if you have them. I use my light camera tripod as a sort of frame, if the pack is heavy. Often, it is sufficient to "think elongated" and pack elongated items vertically inside, instead of horizontally. When everything has been packed, it is important to compress the back area well. This gives you a reasonably stiff contraption that makes weight transfer to the waist belt possible.

This weight transfer to your hips is essential. Do not mistake the packs I am describing here for ordinary day packs of the same size. These are usually not constructed for weight transfer, but are made to be carried with your shoulders only. The belt is there to keep it from flopping, not to transfer weight to your hips. Weight transfer to your hips is important for packs made for longer hikes.

You can easily find packs that weigh three, four or five kilos (7-11 lbs) on the market. The heaviest seem to be 130 litre (8,000 cu inches) packs with military connotations, in which Special-Forces soldiers can carry their personal gear as well as ammunition, explosives and other equipment that brings the weight up to 40-50 kilos (90-110 lbs) or more. But for hiking you can buy a pack that is considerably cheaper and use the money you save for tickets and food for another week or two of hiking.

I can repeat forever that you can save a lot of weight by choosing a light pack. The backpack belongs to the three big ones and merits a lot of attention. Certainly, you also have to have light gear to put in it. If you are an experienced backpacker you will have no problems with a frameless pack weighing less than 1 kilo (2 lbs 2 oz). The same goes for the less experienced hiker, but if you feel a bit uncertain about what to choose, I recommend a pack with some kind of simple frame, weighing maybe 1,2-1,8 kilos (3-4 lbs). You need nothing sturdier if you are going to carry less than 25 kilos (55 pounds) of gear in it. I believe this plan works for most of us hikers.

Bug
protection

For photos and updates, see
the live part of this book at
www.smarterbackpacking.com

Light and thin clothing made of microfibers give excellent protection against stinging and biting insects. Add an ordinary bug net for your head and you will manage in most situations. A net of that kind will also keep your mouth, nose and ears free from non-biting but annoying little flies and their relatives.

For three-season backpacking you will need little or no protection from our stinging fellow creatures, but vacations for most people means that it is bug season while we are hiking. The need for bug protection is individual. Some people are less pestered than others, and tolerance levels vary as well.

The most important part of the bug protection for hikers is their clothing. The very light and thin microfiber fabrics, which I recommend for both windshirts and pants, have the advantage that the fabrics are so tightly woven that the mosquitoes cannot penetrate.

Mosquitoes are often less of a pest than different varieties, some very small, of biting flies and their brethren. They can be extremely stressful when they enter nostrils, ears and eyes without being bothered by threats or violence. If you hike in an area where you can count on the attendance of these little fellows, a small bug net that covers you from hat to collar is a solution that is both light and right.

A net of that kind weighs around 20 grams (3/4 oz) and can easily be made at home if you wish. It is simply a cylinder of bug proof netting with elastics in seams at both ends. One end goes over your cap, the other fits around your collar or, should you decide to lengthen it a bit, around your shoulders. Nets like this can also be bought ready-made.

There are also bug hats in the stores that will weigh hundreds of grams (5-10 oz). I find them both unnecessary and heavy since I always bring a cap anyway. These hats often have rings sewn into them to create a space between the netting and the skin. I do not find any need for this, as the netting usually is a bit stiff and folds away from the skin if there is a bit of extra fabric. So, in my view, these hats are probably better off on the heads off fly fishermen and hunters who do not travel long distances from house or car.

Personally, I try to avoid chemical warfare with insects, but I do not hesitate to use chemicals if the situation becomes unbearable. There are few substances that actually have scientifically proven themselves effective against bugs, and DEET is the classic one. My own experiences of other substances are limited. There are many concoctions, some local, some ecological and some using ancient recipes. Most of them have not shown any repelling effects in tests, so I stay away from them.

I prefer to carry my repellent as a solid stick similar to antiperspirant dry sticks, since I find it easier to transport and easier to apply.

There are other types of bugs as well in different parts of the world, which the hiker may encounter. Covering all types of terrain in all countries is beyond the scope of this book. However, I will say something briefly about ticks.

You can treat loosely woven garments, like merino shirts and socks, with pyretroids, which are insecticides. This kills or hurts the insects (DEET just confuses their ability to find blood-filled creatures). I do not like bringing an insecticide in direct contact with my skin. So, for my upper body I prefer using the windshirt as protection. For feet and ankles a pyretroid might be the only solution in some areas. Then, tuck the bug-proof microfiber into your socks and with that, you have done all you can do.

You can save quite a bit of weight by using a small head net instead of a bug hat, but for most people there is not that much weight to save on bug protection. However, do not bring more equipment than you need. A stick of DEET lasts me several weeks, but this is an individual matter and is of course also dependent on terrain and season. Furthermore, several people can of course share a stick.

Camera

For photos and updates, see
the live part of this book at
www.smarterbackpacking.com

The small and handy digital cameras of today make it possible for most of us to manage with a camera weighing less than 200 grams (6.5 oz). Heavier equipment usually means that for you, photography is an important hobby.

.

The camera is not really necessary for hiking, unless you are a professional photographer. Still, most of us carry some kind of camera, and some amateurs carry more gear than professionals. Here we are entering an area of personal choice: for some people the hike is just a necessary evil in order to access interesting photographic motifs. I am not competent to give advice on photographic equipment for people in this category. I can only suggest that if the part of the pack that is not photographic gear is as light as possible, this will increase mobility and enjoyment as well as create space for even more lenses or other camera gear.

For the more average holiday snap shooter I can present my solution for photographic equipment. I write books and magazine articles where I publish some pictures, like in this book or on the web. Still, I would not consider myself a skilful photographer, and the camera I mostly use is a compromise. It is a small digital camera with a zoom from medium wide angle to medium telephoto lens, or 1X-3X. It weighs slightly less than 200 grams (6.5 oz). A telephoto lens equalling 3X is perhaps the most useful for snapping pictures of mountains without having them look uninterestingly small, instead of using 1X or 2X.

The camera can be pushed to perform even outside these limits with digital, not optical, means which will equal longer telephoto lenses. However, you pay a price in lower quality. If you use a tripod, you can still get decent photos of animals and the like, that are good enough for your album or for family picture shows.

The technical development in cameras is very rapid; especially if you look at the ones living inside the gadgets most of us still call mobile phones. I imagine that mobile phones will soon have a capacity that makes a separate camera unnecessary for the average photographer.

Cameras run on batteries and I have found that these batteries usually lasts me for several weeks, unless I snap many hundreds of pictures every day. Thus, I have not found it necessary to charge them while on the trail. If I am in doubt, I bring two fully charged batteries.

There are solar powered chargers but I see little weight advantage with them. I usually visit small towns and villages every week or so, even on long hikes. For now it seems easier to bring the standard charger for my camera and plug it into the wall somewhere. In order to save weight I have shortened the cord from over 1,000 mm (4 feet) to 250 mm (10 inches), which saves a surprising amount of weight.

My camera always travels in the belt pocket of my pack, usually wrapped in a homemade silnylon bag with thin fleece lining, making it a bit more shock proof and water resistant. The number of good water-proof cameras is on the increase, so maybe I will soon be carrying one of those instead. For me, the most important thing is that the camera is easy to pull out, snap photos with and put back.

A small and light tripod weighing around 150 grams (5 oz) is also part of my equipment. Since I am mostly a solo hiker, I use the tripod in order to place a human being somewhere in the foreground, to add depth and interest to a photo of nature scenery. The tripod is sort of home-made. I have added carbon fiber rods to a table tripod, which makes it about 600 mm (2 feet) high.

In the past, at times I also brought a light camcorder along and used it as a diary. It will be a way to revive old hikes when I get old and will only be able to hike among my memories. But today the feature of moving pictures is usually part of the ordinary camera and we do not need the extra piece of camcorder gear.

There can be considerable differences in weight between light and heavy camera gear, but at the end of the day this is a matter of personal preference.

Caps

For photos and updates, see
the live part of this book at
www.smarterbackpacking.com

Head gear can be life-saving but may suffer from not being trendy in some circles. An ordinary knitted beanie made of wool or synthetics is excellent and need not weigh much. A baseball cap can be a good complement and gives some protection of face and eyes from sun and rain.

The action hero might need to keep his head cool, but for us ordinary mortals it is often more important to keep our heads warm. Your head contains large amounts of fluid and a bunch of essential functions which demands a steady supply of fresh and warm blood.

That is why our heads never feel cold in the same way that our hands feel cold, sometimes painfully cold. The hands are not considered by the organism to be essential for our survival, and circulation to them is frequently restricted when heat management is called for. This also happens to other peripheral parts of the body.

If the circulation to our brain would be restricted in the same way as to our feet, we would rapidly loose consciousness and die. That is why our body keeps on pumping warm blood into our head as long as there is the least chance of survival. The effect of this is that an unprotected head will give off heat like a water-filled radiator. Sometimes, for example, when we are too hot, this is helpful, at other times it can be lethal.

As most action heroes live in the protected world and climate of Hollywood, they only need to use caps when the director feels like it. So, most of us have grown up with actors in contemporary movies not wearing anything on their heads, and we are influenced by this. That might be one reason that many people, even in my northern country, do not wear any caps even in mid-winter.

So, a warning is in place, do not adhere to the fad of not wearing a cap when you go out into the mountains, where you need one. Nothing is more beneficial and pays better for its weight than a cap, when you are cold and shivering.

The best warm cap I have ever used is a homemade hood or bomber cap made out of thin, ripstop nylon with a thin layer of synthetic insulation. This cap is warm, windproof and weighs around 50 grams (2 oz). Products like that can be found on the market, but because you look like a jerk wearing them, according to today's fads, they are not easy to find. If you are not using a warm jacket with an insulated hood, I recommend a cap like that; a really warm cap, preferably windproof, if you hike in a chilly climate.

I always use a cap when I am sleeping, to keep warm

and also to protect the inside of the sleeping bag from my greasy tendrils. For this reason the cap has to be soft and should fit well on my head in different sleeping positions. An ordinary knitted beanie with a good fit works very well.

However, in the last couple of years I have used an undershirt with a hood for sleeping and left the knitted cap at home. In combination with a hood on your windshirt and/or rain jacket, this will keep your head warm while hiking in any three-season weather.

Extremely warm caps for dog sledders in Alaska can weigh quite a bit, but few would pick them for a three-season hike. So, you will probably not save more than 50-60 grams (2 oz) by choosing a light cap instead of a heavy cap.

One other type of cap is close to my heart – the baseball cap. The main function of this cap is not to keep your head warm, even if it helps doing that too, as it is usually quite windproof. For me, the main function is to shade my eyes instead of or as support for my sunglasses. The cap I am wearing is homemade and has a neck piece that can be let down to give protection against the sun. If you hike a lot in hot and sunny climates this is really a good device. In fact, you might consider using a wide-brim hat instead. With a small and light pack, this works well, while a big pack will bump into the brim at the back of the neck in an annoying manner.

For hot climate, a cotton hat is revered by many, because you can soak it in water and let it cool your head for a while.

Clothing

For photos and updates, see
the live part of this book at
www.smarterbackpacking.com

*The base layer keeps your skin dry, the middle layer
insulates and the outer layer or top layer protects
against wind and precipitation. This is the classic
three layer principle and very important to
understand and use. With this knowledge you can
stay warm and dry even with very light garments, if
you pick the right ones and learn how to use them.*

Dressing in layers is a well established outdoor principle
and the gist of it is that you combine different garments
with different functions to achieve maximum comfort
and safety. It is not really complicated. Usually we dress
more or less like that in everyday life, although we might
not be aware of the theory behind it. However, in order
to be comfortable when you engage in physical activities
outdoors, it is useful to know more about how to adjust
your clothing to the situations you encounter.

Next to your skin you have an inner layer or base
layer – the one we usually call underwear. The base layer

has the primary function to keep your skin dry, which means you will stay warm, by efficiently transporting your body moisture away from the skin surface. Moisture on your skin is very cooling, which is the general idea. Sweating comes from the body needing to regulate its core temperature to the 37 C (98.6 F) that is best for us.

For backpacking and other outdoor activities, a base layer has to be able to manage the changes between physical activity that produces sweat, and longer or shorter periods of sedentary activity, in such a way that the body is not chilled. Management of these changes represents the biggest difference between the purpose of a base layer for backpackers and the base layer for couch potatoes.

I have found it important to focus on moisture transport as being the essential function of the base layer. It is not important, or probably not even desirable that the base layer insulates and helps maintaining body temperature that way. The base layer should make sure that body moisture is not present on the skin surface when your body is active; and should cool the body when not active – when you take a break or sleep.

Now let us examine the middle layer. The name tells where you find it. It is sometimes called the insulating layer. This layer consists of one or several layers outside the base layer with the purpose of preserving body temperature, by insulating. This layer insulates because it contains tiny pockets of still air. The traditional middle layer is a sweater of wool or fleece, or any garment that is fluffy and contains air.

The purpose of the middle layer is that it should neither be used as base layer nor a top layer, because then it is not a middle layer, right? However, there are always garments that do not fit this theory. The down jacket is an example of an insulating layer that is also windproof. Thus, it is a combination of middle/ insulating layer and top layer or shell, if you wear it on top of your windshirt; and a straight middle layer if you wear your windshirt on top of the down jacket. The latter, actually, is a very good idea – it increases the warmth of a down jacket considerably, especially when it is windy.

Typical middle layer garments are down jackets, jackets with synthetic insulation, fleece jackets or wool sweaters. But a second base layer garment, that is identical to the one next to the skin, is by definition a middle layer and serves as insulation in this position, and not as moisture transporter.

Finally, we come to the shell or top layer that serves to protect against wind and rain. This layer is exactly what it says, a shell around your body that helps the clothing underneath to do its job.

The shell should manage the contradiction between protecting you from wind and rain from the outside and letting body moisture from the inside pass through, so that this moisture does not saturate your other layers and begins to chill you. This is pretty tricky indeed, but today we have garments that can do this reasonably well. The most important aspect, though, is that these garments keep moisture from the outside stay on the outside. This is particularly important when you are backpacking in exposed environments like high mountains above timberline, or on tundra.

These excellent materials that are both waterproof and still 'breathe', letting some moisture out, are often called waterproof/breathables. I usually find it easier to call them Mextex. This derives from the fact that most of these fabrics have borrowed the suffix "-tex" from the leading brand GoreTex. And the slight pun of switching the order of the word for the popular Tex Mex kitchen made my day. Of course, not everyone appreciates that you deal with serious matters like waterproof/ breathables in such an offhand way, but what can you do when you prefer smiling from furrowing your brows?

A rainproof garment is of course also windproof, while a windproof garment may not be waterproof. So, some people think one garment is enough – a Mextex shell jacket. I do not agree, because I see no point in using a rain jacket unless it is raining. Even though Mextex garments claim that they breathe and transport moisture, the amount they transport is not that impressive. All right, the garments are better at moisture transport than a plastic bag, but most people tend to become rather soaked inside them if they wear them while exerting themselves.

Hence, in my experience, it is better to have one windproof garment and one rain-proof garment. Strangely enough, a light wind shirt and a light rain jacket often weigh considerably less than most Mextex shell jackets. This is discussed more in detail in the chapters Rain jacket and Windshirt. The base layer and the middle layer also have their own chapters. What you just read is only a general background to the overall clothing system that I advocate.

Compass

For photos and updates, see
the live part of this book at
www.smarterbackpacking.com

*A good compass does not weigh more than 20 grams
(3/4 oz), but there are even lighter variants if you
follow trails and do not need to plot a course.*

The compass is seldom left behind when I am hiking,
even if I can manage without it in theory, if I am simply
following trails. The low weight in combination with the
safety it brings makes it seem like a good investment.
Some compasses weigh only a couple of grams (1/10 oz)
and there are those that weigh more than 100 grams (3
oz), and most of them are somewhere in between.

I am using a fairly ordinary compass with a mirror. I
would not go very far without a base plate compass, but
that is probably a matter of habit. I am used to it and can
easily plot a course and get my bearings by sighting
distant mountains and the like. Wrist compasses are in
my view more difficult to use, as are the even smaller
compasses you find in key rings.

The compass I use is a sighting compass with a mirror,
another useful item. The compass weighs around 20

grams (3/4 oz). It has the basic functions of a compass and can be attached to my clothing with a safety pin, which gives me both hands free to hold my poles when hiking or skiing.

You can find very advanced compasses on the market, that enable you to measure the decline of avalanche prone slopes, and that have a number of different scales. However, for the hiking that I do, a pretty basic compass is good enough. The mirror is a help when combing or shaving, so it is well worth the extra weight.

When you only hike along well marked trails, and if you have little interest in identifying surrounding hills and mountains, you do not really need much of a compass. The compass is mainly a tool to be used when visibility is poor and in some emergency situations. In such situations, it is of course important that you have some basic skills in handling the compass.

You can save 100 grams or more (3-4 oz) by picking one of the lighter compasses instead of a heavier one. The experienced hiker can probably do well with a really light compass, but, on the other hand, may have more complex route finding needs than the inexperienced hiker.

Cooking

For photos and updates, see
the live part of this book at
www.smarterbackpacking.com

You can save several hundred grams (5-10 oz) or more, depending on the type of heat source you choose for your cooking. For most solutions however, the difference in weight is slight and the very lightest are in my opinion mostly for enthusiasts in benign climates. A simple and functional solution need not be heavy. My personal favorite at the time of writing (2010) is the top mounted canister stove. A windscreen is an important addition for securing good fuel economy.

In this chapter I will describe the equipment needed for a hot meal. "Stove" or "kitchen" could also be used as heading. Related information can be found under the chapter heading Light my fire, which mainly informs readers about open fire. Details about cooking gear are found under the witty heading Cooking pots and such.

I know backpackers who skip all cooking gear and manage well with different kinds of cold food, which saves weight. Personally, I belong to the majority of hikers who want hot food several times a day, and who also consider the meals to be some of the highlights of the day. But this does not mean that my equipment for heating food is particularly heavy.

Basically, I need something that allows me to bring water to the boil. If I want to save fuel I do not even have to bring it to a boil. With hot or boiling water I can fix my hot drinks and hot food.

Furthermore, I want a stove that can be used inside my tent or right close outside, so that I can cook while lying in my sleeping bag under a roof when it is rainy and windy or the bugs are a menace. Words of warning are often heard about using gear that produce carbon monoxide inside tents. This should be considered but not to the point where people get panic-stricken. All my own experience and what I have read indicates that you do not have to worry about this in a normal, ventilated tent without snow cover.

Usually, I am careful and put my stove outside the foretent or in an open foretent if this is possible, without any worries. There does not seem to be any singular case of carbon monoxide deaths in tents in the United States that could be blamed on a hikers' stove. From what I have read, reported cases of poisoning stems from people at campgrounds using burners or barbeques, that were left burning all night, as a heat source, often in combination with snowfalls during the night that restricted the ventilation.

I have used alcohol stoves like Trangia for decades before I actually put it on a scale and found that it weighed 1,100 grams (2 lbs 7 oz). Now, this includes pots and frying pan as well as windscreen; but the clincher was that I discovered that the lid/frying pan weighed 200 grams (7 oz). Since I never fried anything, I replaced it with a piece of foil weighing next to nothing. Today there are lighter versions of the Trangia, but also a huge amount of other stoves, some heavy and some light.

The way I see it there are four sources of heat for your food that are light enough for 3-season backpacking:

• Canister gas
• Alcohol
• Solid fuel
• Wood

I guess I listed them in the order of my preference, so I will discuss them in the opposite order to compensate for this.

From a weight point of view, the open fire might be lightest solution, but heavy when it comes to skill. It is difficult and takes a lot of practice to be able to light a fire in ANY kind of weather. Once, many years ago, I made a late fall hike in a pine forest, and even in this favorable ecosystem I did not have as many hot meals as I had wished for...

Almost as good as open fires are the small and usually brilliantly concocted metal containers for burning twigs. The kind of kindling they require can often be found even above the timberline, and these tiny stoves are easier to light and use than an ordinary camp fire. But they do weigh a bit and often more than other kinds of burners, so a lot of the weight advantage is lost. Their real strength is on really long and unsupported hikes, because you do not have to carry fuel. However, these stoves flame up and gives off smoke and soot to such an extent that I do not want to use them in a foretent.

Wood is of course a form of solid fuel, but in this context solid fuel means tablets based on alcohol or other substances. Esbit is a common brand. Theoretically, weight for weight, solid fuel is probably the lightest cooking solution for backpackers. A piece of metal the size of a teaspoon, a pot support and a windscreen is all you need, and these can be very light.

My own limited experience of solid fuels is that they work reasonably well when the weather is benign. They are used by many American ultralight backpackers, often in drier and warmer weather than the more maritime, cold and damp weather that I am more used to. However, I think you risk having to wait a bit too long for your hot meal when using solid fuel in cold, wet and windy weather.

You can take an alcohol burner from a complete kitchen like the Trangia and use the burner separately. You can put the burner between a couple of rocks and place the pot on top, or better, buy or make a simple pot support and windscreen. This brings the weight down considerably. That is how I started going lightweight in the kitchen department.

The handy man can make his own alcohol burner from old soda cans. An abundance of constructions and instructions is available on the Internet. These burners weigh 15-30 grams (0.5-1 oz) and on a good day they may work almost as well as a traditional Trangia burner or similar, that weighs around 100 grams (3-4 oz).

Nowadays, my personal favorite is the kind of light gas burners that you attach directly on top of a gas canister. These burners from Primus, Optimus or MSR top the scales at 60-100 grams (2-3 oz) including pot support. Fitted with a Piezo ignition they are extremely easy to use and will produce hot water very quickly even if it is cold, wet and windy. Their only setback is that they tend to be a bit unstable on uneven surfaces, but usually you can find a reasonable spot for keeping them balanced. As far as I can remember, I have only tipped a kettle over once on that kind of a stove. Not fun, but most of the food was salvageable, and in my view, the advantages with these stoves outweigh such setbacks.

A fifth type of fuel is petroleum-based, white gas and kerosene. They demand special types of stoves where you pressurize the fuel. You end up with fairly heavy contraptions. You can often use white gas and kerosene and also diesel and what not in these multi-fuel stoves.

The tank for the pressurised fuel and the hose connecting this to the burner tend to add at least 100-200 grams (3-6 oz). In my view, they are mainly stoves for extremely cold winter trips. I have used my top mounted canister stove in temperatures down to -20 C without problems, as long as I kept the canister in my pocket or sleeping bag. These stoves can also be used for travelling in parts of the world where your favorite fuel might not be at hand and you have to make do.

However, if you already have that kind of a stove you

do not lose more than 100-200 grams (3-6 oz) compared with the lightest solutions. And you can often use gas canisters as well for these stoves, so if you manage the 343 or 3 kilos for the three big ones, this is a minor deviation.

No matter what type of fuel or burner you use, protection from wind is very important. You can read more about that in the chapter Windscreens.

The experienced backpacker might enjoy experimenting with different types of home-made burners from soda cans, or different solid-fuel solutions. However, you do not save many grams (tenths of oz) from this. For the less experienced I recommend a safer and duller technology, like top mounted canister gas stoves or commercial alcohol stoves. You do not gain much weight with that, and you have found a solution that is reliable and handy in most circumstances. Foolproof is the established expression, and the discerning reader is thus made aware of why I prefer that type of stove.

Cooking pots and such

For photos and updates, see
the live part of this book at
www.smarterbackpacking.com

*It is easy to bring lots of neat utensils for cooking
and eating. However, pot, cup and spoon from light
materials are really all you need.*

Reducing the weight of kitchen utensils is dependent on
the same methods as usual; limiting the number of
things you bring and then choosing the lightest models.

For many years I used a Trangia alcohol stove
complete with windscreens, two pots and a frying pan.
To this I had also added a small brush, a small whisk and
a small spatula. After a couple of decades I realized that
I never used the spatula and removed it. The whisk kept
going along until I realized that I seldom had any use for
it and that the spoon then worked just as well.

I have harder to forgive myself for not extending the
spatula logic of never frying anything to exclude the
frying pan. This was probably because I used it all the
time as a lid for my pots. This went on until the day
when I started doing something serious about my pack.

51

using the 343 method (in its infancy) and started weighing all my gear. I then found that the frying pan that I never used for frying weighed 220 grams (7 oz) and that a piece of foil, like in the shape of a pie plate, worked just as well as a pot lid and only weighed 5 grams (1/6 oz).

Today my cooking gear consists of either a light aluminium or titanium pot, weighing around 100 grams (3-4 oz). The aluminium one is a bit larger, with room for slightly more than 1 liter (34 oz), the titanium slightly lighter and holding 0.8 liter (27 oz). The aluminium one is more than 30 years old, which proves that it is pretty difficult to wear out a cooking pot. Pick the lightest and stay away from non-stick coatings (which is not as durable as the pot itself) and the pot will probably last a lifetime.

If you are a solo hiker who really wants to minimize your gear you can pick a pot that is also a cup and holding about 0.6 liter (20 oz). Something like that will have a handle and weigh around 60-70 grams (2-2.5 oz). A bigger pot like the one I am often using plus a handle for it plus a regular cup will weigh around 200 grams (6-7 oz), which means you will save around 4 oz using the ultra light style. I do not think it is worth it, as I like a cup that is separate from the pot, but there are of course very light cups, or you can drink straight from your water bottle.

For washing dishes I manage well without a brush. To use the spoon and some water to scrape most of the remnant food from inside the pot works very well. If necessary I heat the water a bit, and sometimes I use a handful of grass to wipe with. The pot does not need to be completely clean as I will heat water in it for my next meal and this will disinfect it. If I am really pressed by dirty pots I can use some of the soap I have in my hygiene department. I never bring detergent; I have simply no use for it.

You can save quite a bit of weight by choosing light kitchen gear and probably more by leaving most of the neat gadgets at home (or preferably in the store).

Cup

For photos and updates, see
the live part of this book at
www.smarterbackpacking.com

An ordinary plastic cup will do very well. There are variants, some lighter and some heavier. I do not use an extremely lightweight cup and thus, I have to accept an extra 30-40 grams (1-1.5 oz) as my cup is better insulated than the lightest versions.

Some people choose insulated cups that weigh several hundred grams (6-8 oz), others manage altogether without a cup. Most of us are likely to choose something in between.

Many light packers use a very large cup that doubles as a cooking pot, or they use a small cooking pot that doubles as a cup. This means metal; in most cases a choice between aluminium or titanium. A stainless steel cup will last a couple of lifetimes and weighs as much as a light down quilt. One person can manage with a cooking pot of around 0.6 liter (20 oz) and these combined cups and pots weigh less than 100 grams (3 oz) including a folding handle.

The cup is a thing of comfort, a luxury item. If you

bring a drinking bottle, you can drink from it while eating from your pot. Or, you do not drink at all while you are eating. Personally, I find that a bit austere, and I feel that my cup is worth its weight.

A very light cup is a plastic or Styrofoam cup that you get at a fast food joint; or you can buy disposable picnic cups. They do not weigh more than 5-10 grams (1/5-1/3 oz) and will probably last you a week or so. Even waxed paper cups are surprisingly resilient and do not crack as easily as plastic ones. My dad once used such a paper cup for more than a week, when he had forgotten to pack his regular cup for a hike. Should a cup like that break, you drink both water and coffee from your pot.

I usually belong to the luxury segment myself; using one of the lightest insulated cups, double wall plastic with a lid. This cup weighs 90 grams (3 oz) – about twice the weight of a single wall plastic cup without a lid, which I also use. I really appreciate coffee that is hot, even after a period of contemplative sipping, so I do feel this luxury is worth the extra weight. And, like many lightweight backpackers, I can afford this, as my pack is so light anyway. The weight of the pack in itself is not the important point, but what you can use the lighter weight for – lighter steps, longer days, more wine, fishing gear, climbing gear or whatever makes life worth living.

Eating utensils

For photos and updates, see
the live part of this book at
www.smarterbackpacking.com

A spoon and a cup is all that is needed if you eat straight from your pot. Combining pot and cup makes utensils even lighter. This both keeps the food warmer and diminishes the dish washing. Plastic or wooden spoons are my favorites.

Usually I eat from the pot and only use a spoon for this. I never felt the need for a fork and a knife. A real knife, not a table knife, is useful to take along for cutting food such as bread, cheese, sausages. Plastic spoons have a tendency to age and weaken and break when you least need it, so I prefer a light wooden spoon. You can make them yourself or they can be bought in stores that trade in wood work and in some other stores.

Titanium spoons are light and durable, but they tend to be hugely expensive. This matters, because spoons are easy to lose in the outdoors when you are not careful. In the wintertime they are actually cold to the touch as well.

If I want to go minimal, I use a small pot that doubles

as a large cup, made of titanium or aluminium. As I often want to drink out of this pot while eating, I use a very light bowl for eating the food I cook. This bowl came along with a supermarket frozen soup purchase and the bowl weighs 17 grams (3/5 oz). The bowl is extremely rugged, constructed to manage temperatures from freezing to boiling, and will last for many trips in my pack. I also use it as a lid for the pot while I am heating the water that will dehydrate my food. As far as I am concerned, there is no need to buy anything more expensive or heavy to eat from, even if the outdoor stores are filled with them.

In fact, here is probably the best advice to save weight that I can give you: leave out as many as possible of those nifty and cute utensils more or less remotely connected with cooking and eating!

Food

For photos and updates, see
the live part of this book at
www.smarterbackpacking.com

*Food that contains enough energy for hiking and
enjoying life weighs a bit, usually between 700-
1,000 grams per person and day, using mostly dry
food. You can not do much to change that, in my
opinion. Using dry food and only taking what you
will consume and maybe a little bit extra, is all you
can do to avoid dead weight. When choosing your
food it is important that you select food that
contains enough energy in the form of
carbohydrates and fat.*

My philosophy when it comes to trail food is that you
should endeavour to eat as many calories as you will
burn during your hike. Hiking is energy-consuming.
You will need to eat plenty, and frequently, in order to
keep your energy and blood sugar levels up, so that you
will enjoy your trip and make wise decisions when
necessary.

Of course I recommend that you use dried food as
much as possible. Today even regular supermarkets
offer many choices. Adding some freeze-dried foods

from the outdoor store will give you all you need without weighing you down.

A rule of thumb says that for a man, his food and fuel will weigh closer to 1,000 grams (around 2 lbs) per day while hiking. Women and older persons, as well as smaller persons, need less calories and might get away with 600-700 grams (20-25 oz) per person and day.

The most important thing for me while hiking is that I get enough energy, and the major sources for energy in my pack are fats and carbohydrates. That is just the opposite of what I would choose if I wanted to lose weight, at home. While on a hike for a week or two or three, you do not really have to worry about getting enough proteins, minerals and vitamins. Leave those worries to people on expeditions lasting many months.

Even if food weighs quite a bit, the advantage is that your pack will lighten with up to 900-1,000 grams (around 2 lbs) as the food is consumed. This in combination with using light gear will give some room for luxury items if you like. Fresh fruit and vegetables can be included and consumed during the first part of the trip. Or, why not some wine or whatever will bring a pleasant close to the day, without being essential.

Make sure you do not take along more food than you really need. My way of doing this is packaging almost all food in portions. A box of macaroni is divided into plastic bags with 80-100 grams per person and meal. This also goes for potato flakes, one of my absolute favorites, as it does not even require cooking in order to provide sustenance and can also be mixed with a variety of foods in order to enhance the taste. I often make some sort of mashed potatoes as dinner, two days out of three, and eat a freeze-dried meal the third day. Now everyone knows that my food habits will not result in any stars from gourmet guidebooks. However, both my stomach and my wallet are thoroughly satisfied.

Many books offer abundant information about food in the outdoors, but I will be fairly brief because I think there is usually not much weight to be saved in that area. Using dried food and not carrying more than you need has been done by backpackers for ages.

An abundance of books also concentrate solely on outdoor cooking. Many of these seem to focus more on gourmet cooking using fresh ingredients during short trips, where weight is less of an issue. In these books you will usually find few tips on dried foods for a two-week trip into a wilderness area.

The experienced backpacker probably already has a menu that works well and may be difficult to lighten. For the less experienced hiker my advice is simply: choose dried food containing ample calories in the shape of fats and carbohydrates, and pack it in suitable portions. If your food and fuel weighs more than 900-1,000 grams (2 lbs) per person and day, you should go back and try to bring less food or bring more calorie-dense aliments. And last but not least: choose food that you like and know you will eat. I know from my own experience that high altitudes might cause nausea, and the first food items you will exclude then are the ones you do not feel are tasty.

Footwear

For photos and updates, see
the live part of this book at
www.smarterbackpacking.com

Carrying a weight on your feet takes five times more energy than carrying the same weight on your back. Thus, finding the lightest footwear that does the job has top priority for me. To me, the use of light mesh trail runners has meant less aching feet, less blisters and a lighter step every inch of the way. Getting my feet wet is no big deal as I can don waterproof socks if my feet should get cold. Even though consciously getting your feet wet sounds extreme to some people, looking for the lightest possible footwear makes for a more comfortable hike and less weariness after the day is done.

You may easily forget that your footwear also is something you carry – something that requires energy from your body to be propelled forward. When you make a list of every piece of gear you bring and their weights, you find out that footwear has a substantial weight.

In my pack list, which mainly contains light or very

light gear, my shoes are the heaviest single piece of equipment. The mesh shoes I have favored for the last few years weigh around 740 grams (26 oz) in my size 11. The second heaviest item is my sleeping bag at 685 grams (24 oz). Most traditional hiking boots weigh more than 1 kilo (35 oz) per pair and at times around 2 kilos (70 oz).

Climbers preparing for the first ascent of Mount Everest in 1953 formulated a rule of thumb; one pound on your feet equals five pounds on your back. In other words, to move something attached to your feet requires five times the amount of energy that it takes to transport the same weight on your back.

Since then quite a bit of research supports this rule of thumb. Depending on circumstances such as speed, slope and weight carried, there is of course variation. The US Army has published research that shows a weight increase span of 3.5-5.25 times. Research done by Stephen Legg and others, published in Ergonomics 1986, indicates that carrying a weight on your feet requires 6.4 times the energy output compared to carrying that weight on your back.

Researchers have studied field and track long distance runners to find explanations for why East African runners are so good. This research has shown that there are genetic differences between people from Kenya, Tanzania and some other countries in East Africa and other Africans and Europeans. The East Africans have a thinner and lighter bone structure in their feet and lower legs. So it takes less energy for them to move their feet than it does for us club-foots.

The mechanics behind this are not simple, but an amateur like yours truly can understand that walking and running necessitates that you move your feet vertically, against gravitation, even if the purpose only is motion on a horizontal level. Your upper body, including the pack, however, moves very little vertically when you are walking horizontally. There is also a leverage effect. Having a weight at the far end of a lever, like your leg, makes it more energy-consuming to lift your foot than if the lever had been shorter or nonexistent.

Not only the energy expenditure makes me advocate lighter and more supple footwear for hiking, than what has been the norm for a long time. Stiff and heavy boots seldom give our feet and lower legs an opportunity to bend and move in the way they were created to move. They were created to walk barefoot. The restrictions often lead to diverse ailments, from blisters to aches, in the feet and lower legs.

Somehow, many of us backpackers made the assumption that this is the way it has to be. I have thought that carrying a heavy load also requires heavy and sturdy footwear, which in turn means aching feet and legs. I thought this was because I was not used to hiking long distances and carrying a pack. Nowadays I tend to think that the boots themselves contribute, maybe considerably, to my weary feet at day's end.

One aim of this book is to make clear that heavy packs and heavy boots are not a natural law for backpacking. For 6-7 years now, on some long and strenuous hikes, I have done a lot better with a much lighter pack than I ever thought possible. I have also done better with light shoes than I ever thought was possible – in fact, a great deal better than with heavier footwear. Many hikers have similar experiences.

Fortunately, the market for light and quick-drying trail running shoes has expanded explosively in recent years. At the time of writing (2010) there is much more to choose from for the lightweight packer, than there was only a couple of years ago. In fact, there is such a wide choice that choosing can be difficult.

With the huge amount of choices available, a book like this can only offer general advice. To start with, you have to count on getting your feet wet while hiking. Especially if you hike in arctic or sub-arctic areas most of the time, like I do. But this is not as big a problem as most of us imagine before we try it. As long as you are on the move, your feet stay warm most of the time.

However, you must be able to keep your feet warm in circumstances when wet feet tend to become cold feet. More on this subject can be found in the Socks chapter. As for the shoes, they should soak up and retain minimal amounts of water when they get wet. Remember that water is heavy and it is very energy-consuming to carry heavy weight on your feet.

You might think that waterproof shoes with membranes, of the Mextex variety, should be useful, but I do not agree. (See the Clothing chapter for 'Mextex'.) Trail runners with these membranes protect your feet initially and in circumstances where you do not risk getting into water over the upper rim of the shoe, like on sidewalks. But if you are hiking in the wilderness, you will not be able to avoid getting water into your shoes. Even walking in a lasting rain shower on a sidewalk means that water running down your legs will eventually make your feet wet.

In my opinion, waterproof membranes in your shoes only stop the inevitable water from draining away from them, once it has entered. The membrane will also hinder the drying of shoes and socks. Instead I prefer shoes that are mostly made from mesh, where the water can freely run in and out. They should also contain minimal amounts of padding that soaks up water and retains it longer than necessary.

Thus, I am an advocate of the wet foot principle and claim that wet feet is no problem as long as your feet stay warm. If you get cold feet you need waterproof socks and insulating socks underneath those. This means that the size of the shoes has to accommodate thick as well as thin socks reasonably well. So, when I find a pair of mesh water sport shoes or trail runners that look suitable, I test if they can be used with really thin nylon socks (or barefoot) as well as with insulating socks plus waterproof socks. Shoes that are flexible enough for this are not always easy to find, but one way to increase their roominess is to take out the innersole when you are using the thickest sock combination.

Nowadays I rarely need the thick socks. Around 90% of my hiking, even in what the British would call 'inclement weather' is done in really thin socks and damp shoes, and it works better for me than any other solution I have found during four decades of backpacking. I also found that my shoes seldom (except for longer stretches of hiking off trail on steep slopes) need to be tied particularly tight. In fact, shoes that are close to falling off most of the time seem to give my feet a natural way of movement that keeps them from acquiring blisters or starting to ache after a long day hiking in strenuous terrain.

But this is me. If there is one thing that is very personal, it is what kind of shoes fit a certain pair of feet, or, what we believe will fit our feet. Some people have long, thin feet, others have short and chubby ones. Some people pronate, some people supinate. Some have strong ankles and some have weak ones. You cannot offer specific advice and claim that it will fit everyone, because it will not.

Thus, I write solely about my experiences. You have to get your own. For several years, while covering thousands of kilometres, I have used water sport shoes for hiking. The uppers are mainly mesh and the soles provide a good grip on wet rock. Experts often claim that these shoes are not made for hiking and are not suitable. As long as my feet stay fit in them and I can walk 500 kilometers (310 miles) through the mountains and forests of northern Sweden using them, I tend to neglect such comments. I notice that the same experts claim that you need 2 kilo (4 lb) hiking boots for 'demanding hikes in demanding terrain' and that every other kind of footwear is unsuitable, because it was not made for backpacking. So far, I have found little evidence that this is not just a sales pitch that has been around for so long that magazines and writers of hiking books tend to look at it as the whole truth and nothing but the truth.

So, my advice is: Try something light on your feet. There are in fact very light boots available today, if you think that changing to trail runners is a bit dramatic and extreme. But give light trail runners or mesh shoes a try. You can take them along as extra camp shoes and try to hike in them as well. If it works, fine. If not, you have your regular footwear in your pack. That is how I started, and pretty soon I realized that even though carrying heavy boots in the pack is a lot smarter (5 times smarter) than carrying them on my feet, I simply did not need them.

Sandals are an alternative type of footwear along the same lines. Many people swear by them. I have not used sandals for hiking because the sandals I have come across have been surprisingly heavy. This may change and sandals may become a viable alternative if they are made as light as my mesh shoes. I also prefer the protection that mesh provides, from sharp twigs, which you can encounter while bushwhacking.

Some hikers have skipped shoes and hike barefoot; and you can find shoes that mimic walking barefoot, which may be an alternative worth checking out. I imagine that these shoes take a while getting used to, so my advice is to try these at home, before you go off on a long hike. In fact, some research on shoes and feet has recently surfaced, not popular among most shoe manufacturers, which claims that modern shoes, while protecting the feet in some ways, might also cause long term damage to legs and feet. This is an area worth watching and keeping an eye on with an open mind.

The habit to systematically choose wet feet takes a bit of mental adjustment for most of us. This includes even experienced hikers who know that their feet tend to get wet in some circumstances no matter what they do. Yet, it is well worth trying. And if you feel that it is too extreme and you want to stay with something more traditional, do not forget: Weight. Be ruthless in your search for the lightest available footwear that is compatible with your feet.

You can save kilos ((several lbs) by choosing light instead of heavy footwear. Furthermore, you can multiply the weight difference by a factor 5 to see how much lighter your step and your hike will be.

Fuel transport

For photos and updates, see
the live part of this book at
www.smarterbackpacking.com

*If you need to transport liquid fuel, an ordinary pop
bottle (PET-bottle is usually the lightest and
cheapest solution.*

Often you cannot choose how to transport your fuel.
Fuel can be solid, liquid and gaseous. Solid fuels like
tablets or wax do not really need any special or heavy
containers. Gas comes with its own pressurized canister.
So, it is mostly when we use liquid fuel like alcohol,
kerosene or white gas that alternative containers could
be an issue.

You do not want these liquid fuels on the loose in
your pack; thus, a basic function is that the container
absolutely does not leak. This has led to a whole
assortment of robust and heavy containers for transport
of liquid fuel being available on the market. You can
find lots of more or less sturdy metal containers in
different sizes and colors, for different purposes. The
prices are often high.

In my experience, ordinary soda pop bottles made of

plastic are both tight and sturdy enough. They are also much cheaper and lighter than the metal containers. You can fairly easily find a size that is optimal for the amount of liquid you need for a particular length of trip.

If you have a stove that depends on using a metal bottle for pressurized liquid fuel, like white gas or kerosene, you should pick the very smallest bottle necessary. If the fuel you will need for a particular length of trip does not fit into this metal container you just put the surplus fuel in a pop bottle. You will find more details of my advice regarding these kinds of stoves in the chapter Stoves.

You can often save hundreds of grams (tens of ounces) by choosing a light container for your fuel instead of a heavy one.

Gloves

For photos and updates, see
the live part of this book at
www.smarterbackpacking.com

*A pair of thin, fast-drying fleece gloves is well worth
its weight. Plain fleece without any membranes dry
out faster. These gloves are my all-round choice for
summer and winter trips.*

I would never go into the mountains of Scandinavia at
any time of the year without a pair of gloves, even
though I know that a pair of spare socks can be used on
my hands, as well, in an emergency. There may be
mountains with less inclement weather, but in most
places above timberline you can expect low
temperatures, rain or even snow at any time of year.
After hiking a whole day in rain, most gloves, including
so called waterproof ones, will be wet.

Fairly thin fleece gloves work best for me. I use them
all year round. I have tried gloves with different kinds of
wind or (more or less) waterproof membranes and
found them wanting. They are usually great as long as
they are dry, but when they get wet, the membranes
become a hindrance to quick drying. Even when by a fire,
I have had problems getting these gloves to dry out. The
ordinary fleece ones without membranes dry much faster.

My thin fleece gloves weigh around 35 grams (1 ¼ oz). Even slightly heavier ones give a good optimization of warmth and dexterity. An important feature of your gloves is that they should let you handle your gear while wearing them, when needed. Naturally, this is particularly important in the winter, when I usually wear a pair of heavy mitts on top of my gloves.

For summer and especially for fall use, I often also put a pair of homemade, leaf-thin mitts in my pack. They are made out of silnylon and weigh around 10 grams ((2/5 oz). They are windproof and fairly waterproof (I have not bothered sealing the seams), which can be really nice in soggy and chilly weather with cold winds. However, I usually manage with only the fleece gloves. A couple of spare plastic bags or empty food bags can be used as mitts in an emergency.

Most of the time, my fleece gloves keep my hands warm enough while I am hiking, even if they are soaked by rain. When I stop for the night, I easily wring them semi-dry (much more difficult if they have membranes) and stow them in my pant pockets to dry out a bit. After camp chores, the gloves can migrate into my sleeping bag and are usually completely dry in the morning. If they are too wet to put in the sleeping bag, I hang them to dry in my tent and put them on damp in the morning if necessary.

You can save 50-100 grams (2-3 oz) by choosing this kind of light gloves, which also give good dexterity for handling gear, instead of large and bulky gloves or mitts that may or may not be as waterproof as claimed.

GPS

For photos and updates, see
the live part of this book at
www.smarterbackpacking.com

*A GPS (Global Positioning System) receiver can at
the moment of writing (2010) not replace map and
compass for cross country hiking. Some time in the
future it probably will. If you do not choose to leave
your GPS at home I recommend picking one of the
simplest and lightest you can find, as the most
important function of a GPS is that it enables you
to get an accurate fix on your position.*

The question to ask is not whether route finding using
the Global Positioning System will replace map and
compass. The question is, when? So far the answer is: not
yet.

As far as I can see, GPS receivers are not yet reliable
enough or energy-saving enough for anyone to leave
map and compass at home; possibly if you travel along
well marked trails, but not for cross country hiking. This
makes the GPS a tool that is useful but not necessary.
You can choose to leave it at home (or in the store). The
more advanced gadgets are mostly for fun, which means

that I have saved ounces and more importantly, lots of money, by not buying one.

In my view, we want to focus on the function that is *unique* to a GPS, rather than the functions that can replace map and compass. The most important function is that the GPS can give an very reliable fix on your position, no matter what the weather is like or how dark it might be.

Before I take off on a hike, I always enter the positions of cabins, bridges and other features on my GPS. That way I know I will find the cabin, even if visibility is near zero. Likewise, you can enter the position of your camp on your GPS if you go on day trips, like hiking up on a peak. You can leave most of your gear in camp and still feel secure that you can find it again.

I mostly use my GPS receiver while navigating by dead reckoning, which can happen in poor weather with limited visibility. Hiking in fog in hilly areas makes it difficult to judge speed and how far I have walked, even if I can be reasonably sure of my direction because of my compass. But as long as I have a known starting point, say, where I was when the fog came, or where my tent was in the morning when I started hiking, I can get a good fix on my position even in fog. Because I know my compass course and I know the distance from my present position to where I started on this course, it is easy to calculate where I am on a straight line on the map.

Knowing my position is an important safety aspect, both physically and mentally. When hiking in fog or rain that limits visibility, it is important for my mental balance to feel that I am in control of certain matters; to know where I am and how quickly I travel.

You can save 100 grams (3-4 oz) or more by skipping one of the heavier GPS receivers and instead picking one of the lighter models.

Hygiene

For photos and updates, see
the live part of this book at
www.smarterbackpacking.com

*Since childhood we are influenced by advertising for
different kinds of hygiene products, and we do not
think we can manage without them. But we can. A
toothbrush and a small chunk of soap will cover all
rational needs for hygiene.*

Hygiene is an area where a huge amount of money is
invested in advertising in order for us to feel inadequate
and unattractive. There would not be much left of
newspapers and magazines if the soap, shampoo,
toothpaste and detergent ads disappeared.

These massive amounts of money spent over decades
have of course influenced billions of people,
unfortunately including you and me. This makes it very
difficult if one should question, which I am about to do,
the necessity of treating body, hair and teeth with
chemical solvents a number of times every day.

I have in fact discovered that when I raise this little
question mark, many people come down on me like a
ton of bricks. Words like "disgusting" and worse are

pretty common.

My opinion is in short: Water is a marvellous substance in many, many ways. One of them is that almost all substances are soluble in water. This is so natural for us that we mostly tend to think of things that are not water-soluble, when it comes to cleaning.

When we are out hiking we are mostly exposed to"clean" dirt that is water-soluble. Anything that is potentially pathogenic is almost always something we take along ourselves. And if not, it is usually pretty obvious that we should avoid it both by its looks and smell. Faeces and decaying animal corpses are examples.

Thus, I use cold water straight from lakes or creeks to take care of most of my hygienic needs while hiking. I brush my teeth with water and toothbrush. A week or two in the woods without toothpaste will not add to my dental decay or make my breath smell worse than usual.

I wash my hands and face every day, even if it is really cold, and on warm and sunny days I might take a bath or wash armpits and groin area. If the dirt is reluctant to leave, I add soap or heat the water a bit, which usually takes care of most kinds of dirt on my skin.

Grease and fat are not water-soluble, but if I get butter or organic oil on my skin, that is no big problem. If I get it on my clothing there will be stains. This is usually only an aesthetic problem that will go away in my washer, when I am back home.

I try to avoid chemical solvents. They tend to be harmful to the environment where they are used and they weigh in my pack. The only item I take with me is a small piece of soap, about as big as the tip of my thumb. To me a piece of hard soap is much easier to take along than liquid soap. You do not need a safe container that does not leak and you do not unnecessarily carry water.

I often only use my soap when returning to civilization and having that glorious, first hot shower. The soap will dissolve the grease in my hair just as well as it dissolves the grease on my skin, so I do not need the specialized solvent known as shampoo. Washing my hair with soap a couple of times every now and then will not kill me nor will it make me bald. I also manage very well without any towel, see the chapter Towel.

I clean my cooking and eating utensils with cold water and scrape them reasonably clean, usually with my spoon. Sometimes I use a bit of soap. After a couple of rinses my cooking pot is clean enough to go in the pack. The next time I use it I will boil whatever residue is left in it and this will be enough to keep me from getting sick. I do not say it will kill any bacteria that might have grown there since my last meal, but for practical purposes in the cool environments where I hike it is enough. I have never become sick while hiking. In fact, my pot seldom needs any cleaning at all, as I often only boil water in it, which I then add to food I eat in other containers, some which are disposable.

If for some reason I cannot get these utensils clean with only water, I do not need any special dish-washing chemicals. The piece of soap is still just as good at dissolving grease and dirt, and is concentrated and easy to transport.

My clothes very seldom need to be washed while I am hiking. If I am on a very long hike, I usually get new supplies every week, and these supply stops usually give me a chance to do some laundry. If not, most of my clothes are made of thin and quick drying synthetics and I can then use a sunny day to wash them in cold water and let them dry on my pack. My merino clothing that I wear next to my skin is less quick drying but also seldom needs to be washed. A week or two in a merino shirt and shorts is nothing to worry about; they do not even smell bad the way synthetics tend to do.

If I feel that for a couple of days or weeks I simply cannot manage without a number of chemical-technical products that I have (pardon the pun) been brainwashed to need, I can go back to rule number one: Do not take along more than you will use.

Do not take a whole bar of soap if you can cut off a corner. Do not take 300 grams (10 oz) of shampoo or detergent, instead, pour a small amount into light (put them on your scale) plastic bottles with good screw caps.

Something that should be self-evident but unfortunately is not to everyone is this: Please do not rinse soapy objects directly in a water course. The mountain creek is not a wash basin. Take your water from it and then do your cleaning elsewhere. Dirty water can be poured out onto biologically active soil (not bare sand or gravel, but where things grow) away from open water courses. Few experiences are more disgusting than bending to fill your cup in a crystal clear stream and finding half of someone's serving of macaroni resting on the bottom, like worms in a carcass. Yes, this has happened to me.

At this point let us talk about intestinal infections. Parasites like Giardia are serious problems to hikers in many countries. This is particularly common in areas where many people move about, especially if there also is livestock around like cows and sheep.

This book is not a full-fledged handbook on this subject. If you believe infections are a danger where you are hiking, I suggest you read one of the standard handbooks on backpacking or specialized books on the subject.

However, if you want to save weight, some kind of chemical for purifying water is definitely a better choice than water filters. If you do not have chemicals or filters and come across water that seems suspicious, going on to another water course is always a good idea. Should this not be practical, you can boil the water. This will take care of most parasites, bacteria and viruses.

The greatest danger actually is that you infect yourself. This is believed to be the most common cause of Giardia infections in many areas. It is a fact that the water is not always to blame. After you have defecated you must wash your hands carefully. Cold water can be sufficient, but if you have made more of a mess than usual or want to play it safe in warm climates or where intestine illnesses is common among hiker, soap should be used before you start digging around in your snack bag with your fingers.

If you travel in areas where water is scarce you can

bring a small bottle of gelled alcohol for disinfection of your hands, but soap and water are in fact just as or more efficient as disinfectans.

Toilet paper is in my view a nice thing to have, even if you can use other material to wipe your butt. Leafy plants are often recommended, but in my Scandinavian mountains the leaves are small and often simply needles. Moss can be used, but moss grows very slowly in mountain areas so I do not feel comfortable using moss except in emergencies.

The best and most comfortable replacement for toilet paper is in my mind snow. This might sound very strange, but is in fact not uncomfortable at all. 'Cool' is a more appropriate description, but not chilly in any way. You grab a handful of snow and press it into an oblong shape in your fist. Then you use the pointy end to wipe. Repeat until the oblong is pristine. If the snow is of a consistency that will not let it be shaped in that way, you are shit-out-of-luck!

Many people seem to make do with really small amounts of toilet paper, but I do not. This is something everyone has to research for themselves. However, I do not bring a whole roll. I go into my bathroom, grab one end of the roll and measure up about 1 meter (3 feet) per day. This stretch of tissue I then roll around itself and put in a plastic Ziploc bag together with a small butane lighter of the kind all stores sell to smokers. The lighter is used to set fire to the paper after use. Unless there is a fire hazard of course, or local regulations stipulate that you have to pack it out.

This chapter turned out to be longer than I expected considering my slightly heathen approach to the modern hygiene cult, but this might be all right, as hygienic products can take up a considerable space in many peoples packs. I try to convey a mixture of common sense (you will not die if you do not shampoo your hair every other day) and small package solutions.

My own hygienic gear is a toothbrush for children, a piece of soap weighing 10-20 grams (1/2 oz) and piece of dental floss. A short length of dental floss can be reused for at least three weeks by most people. Just rinse it off like you do with your toothbrush and store the floss in the same plastic bag. If I am carrying more than 100 grams (3 oz) of hygienic products at the trailhead, I would give considerable thought to which psychological and commercial mechanisms rule my life, and ask myself if I really should let them rule.

Knife

For photos and updates, see
the live part of this book at
www.smarterbackpacking.com

*When you do not live off the land, but carry most of
what you need and strive to leave no track, a knife
is no longer the indispensable piece of gear it used to
be. Usually you can manage with a far smaller knife
than you think, or got used to.*

In my younger days, the knife was one of the most
important tools for being outdoors. Old wisdom said:
"If you have no knife, what are you doing in the
wilderness?" For a young guy, there was also magic
involved in owning something that was both a tool and
a weapon. Many knives are aesthetically appealing and it
is no wonder that many people collect knives as a hobby.
Well, I suppose most boys enjoy knives at some stage, as
they grow up.

For people living close to nature and for those living
off the land, the knife is an essential tool that has many
purposes. But for me, who nowadays carry with me
everything I need on my hikes, the need for a knife is
different and more limited. Particularly as I subscribe to

the leave-no-trace ethics. Hence, over the years, my knives have shrunk considerably and migrated from my belt to my pack.

A major factor influencing my choice of knife is whether or not I plan to build a number of fires during a particular hike. If fire is paramount, I need a larger knife. Then I probably need an axe and/or a saw as well.

For summer trips in the far north, where I live, I normally do not need a fire for neither light nor warmth. Fall and winter trips are a different ballgame. During long dark nights a fire is very enjoyable in many ways.

In the summer, I use my knife for some smaller chores – mostly chores like opening food packages, pare off a piece of sausage or cut off some tape for repairs on gear or self. For such tasks you can make do with a very small knife. Some people use a short piece of a utility knife with some tape around. Such an item is almost negligible in weight. As for me, I carry a small Swiss Army knife where the little scissor is used more often than the knife. A pair of tweezers to remove twigs or ticks is part of the same package.

You can save 100-200 grams (3-6 oz) or more by choosing a small and light knife that is adapted to how you actually use your knife in the outdoors. If you really like a large knife, by all means, take it along. At least you have made a conscious decision and do not have to convince yourself and the rest of the world that it is really necessary.

Light

For photos and updates, see
the live part of this book at
www.smarterbackpacking.com

*In my Scandinavian mountains you can manage
without a light most of the time from early summer
to early fall, as it does not get very dark at night. At
other times, a light head lamp with energy-saving
diodes is a good solution. If you want to go minimal,
you can purchase tiny flashlights weighing less than
10 grams (2/5 oz). If you want to use a light while
walking longer distances, you might need a fairly
heavy and potent head lamp.*

For three-season backpacking in the far north, like in
northern Scandinavia, Canada or Alaska, you do not
need any light during much of the season. The end of
August and early September marks the beginning of the
period where it begins to get really dark in the middle of
the night. At other times, there is enough light for you to
read even at two o'clock in the morning. If you are in
doubt, you can check sunrise and sunset data for the area
you are visiting, on the Internet.

It is important that you are clear about the purpose of

your light. Do you need it for hiking in the dark or to be able to find a sock in a dark tent? Walking with a light puts special demands on your tool. The best is a fairly strong head lamp that leaves your hands free and throws a long beam, showing where you can put your feet, or not.

If your needs are minimal, the light can be just as minimal. You can buy key-ring varieties with a single Light Emitting Diode (LED) at most gas stations, which weigh less than 10 grams (2/5 oz) and are powered by a coin-sized battery. If you want a more expensive version you can buy it in the outdoor stores.

The LED lights have revolutionized the lamp industry and more is yet to come. These light bulbs are less expensive, hardier and consume less energy than the old light bulbs. I see no reason to choose anything else.

For hiking you might pick a head lamp with, say, 4-5 LEDs that emit a strong beam. A lamp of this kind weighs around 100-200 grams (3-6 oz). Personally, I have never felt the need for such a lamp. During my army days, we moved around a lot in the dark without using lamps at all, to avoid being seen. So, I know transportation in darkness is quite possible. But if you plan to spend several hours, on a dark autumn night, walking in rough country, a strong head lamp may be worth its weight.

I prefer something in between the lightest and the heaviest, although most of the time I do not bring any lamp at all. For camp chores in the dark – for pitching a tent and the like – I find a light head lamp that frees both my hands for the tasks at hand, to be ideal. If you want to read in your sleeping bag on dark nights, it also comes in handy. Head lamps of this kind weigh from 25 grams (1 oz) and upwards. My own current lamp is a bit ancient and weighs 60 grams (2 oz) but so far I have not found it worth the money to switch to a lighter variety. No doubt, lamps for outdoor activities will get even lighter in the future.

You can save upwards of 250-300 grams (10 oz) by leaving a heavy lamp at home and almost as much by choosing one of the lightest available.

Light my fire

For photos and updates, see
the live part of this book at
www.smarterbackpacking.com

Campfires have a lot to do with emotions. From a safety point of view it is good for a backpacker to always bring some small stuff to make a fire with, if there is no other way to keep warm. Keep in mind that you need a lot of practice to be able to build a fire when you most need it. Matches in a waterproof container are safe and useful to have at hand. Cheap gas lighters from your corner store are also useful. In order to build a fire when most of my gear is wet I also carry a candle stump and some other flammable material.

Few experiences match sitting by a fire on a fall or winter night, while the cold is closing in on the small space of light and warmth created by the golden flames.

My wording in the preceding sentence tells you that campfires trigger emotions. Many people cannot consider camping and hiking without building a fire. This makes fires in the outdoors difficult to discuss, especially in a context where you are supposed to be rational and use a different choice of words to cover up the simple fact: I want to build a fire because I like fires.

I do like fires myself, but I will try to stay away from the emotive aspects of camp fires in this chapter. Nowadays I almost only build fires when I really need the light and the warmth; they are seldom just pleasure fires. I also try to be considerate of people that will arrive to the place where I am camping, after I have left. I can be considerate by building a small fire (and sit close to it), by not building or at least not leaving, fire rings, and by allowing the fire to burn down completely. If there are still some sooty chunks of wood left, I spread them out in the surroundings after making sure that they are completely doused and free of any semblance of sparks.

I build my fire on a surface that will show minimal damage afterwards. Sand and gravel are of course ideal surfaces, but not always available when you need them. However, even on ground with ordinary duff you can minimize the traces you leave. When my fire is out I scrape away all coals and ashes that are loose on the surface and spread them around in bushes or whatever nearby. Left is a small patch of burned soil that will be completely covered by plants in a year or two. This I know from places where I have returned.

From unsavoury fire places I have come across, I have learned that I should not try to burn aluminized packages. The minority of backpackers that have not understood this are much too noticeable.

Fire circles made of rocks can be motivated sometimes, for example, when you teach inexperienced people to use fires or when you are at a base camp where you spend a lot of time. Or, of course at fire pits built for that purpose. Though, it should be noticed that people who live with fire in the wilderness, like the native Sami in my part of the world, do not build any fire rings for temporary cooking fires. Fire rings are probably a heritage from the scout movement, if I dare make a guess. In any event, the main point is, even if I have good reasons for building a fire ring, there is absolutely no reason to leave these stone monuments behind when I move on.

Leaving fire rings is quite simply a form of littering, even if the rings are made by material from the site itself. Most national parks have rules against moving rocks and engaging in other more or less severe forms of "landscaping." In spite of this, you will find many abandoned fire rings where hikers are on the move, even in national parks and other protected areas. You will often also find abandoned tent rings, with rocks used to anchor tent pegs in high winds.

All these rings have in common that they do not go away by themselves until we enter the next ice age. Chopped down trees grow back, aluminium packages are obliterated by time, but rocks of that size remain as monuments of someone's lack of consideration. Let us show consideration for other people coming to the same place after us. They would also like to experience that place as virgin as possible.

My suggestion is that we unite, all of us who wish for our children to have access to a natural world as unspoilt as we can possibly allow it to be. Once or twice daily during our hikes, let us take a couple of minutes to dismantle the fire rings or tent rings that we haphazardly find in our vicinity. Furthermore, if we do need to build fire rings or anchor our tent pegs in a storm, let us endeavor to pick our rocks from the bottom of a creek and return them there when they are no longer needed.

Okay, now that I got that out of my system, let us go back to the subject – building a fire – this time unemotionally, from a safety point of view.

The gear of a modern backpacker should be adapted to operations without fires. Exceptions can be found in the chapter Cooking. But emergencies may occur when neither you nor your gear, maybe due to your gear being wet, can keep you from exposure to hypothermia and danger of death, without the aid of an external heat source.

In such a situation you need a good working knowledge of how to build a fire, know how to build it in different conditions, mostly soggy ones, and know about a couple of important tools. These tools are there to give you a starting point, to provide something that will create a flame of sufficient strength and length of time for you to be able to ignite kindling from the surroundings. A flame stronger and longer lasting than a match or a lighter is needed. If you have a working canister stove, you are in effect in possession of a welding torch that can dry out and set fire to the soggiest kindling. This is true for most stoves you might take along.

If I plan to build a lot of fires on a trip, I take with me a good size patch of dry birch bark as a fire lighter. I also take a small hatchet or a larger size knife than usual. This can amount to a considerable weight in my pack, so for summer trips I never take these items. If I have to build a fire, I can do it without this heavy gear, and when I do not need a fire, they are unnecessarily heavy. I know, because I have carried good size axes and saws around for many years, in my younger days.

I prefer ordinary matches for fire making and have done so for decades. A box in my pocket, wrapped in a plastic bag, has never become wet or let me down for the last 40 years. It would probably not withstand a regular bath, so I always bring a second matchbox in my pack. This box is sealed "bombproof" in thick layers of heat-sealed plastics or firmly taped plastic bags. I have only needed to use this backup once during all these years.

Nowadays I prefer to cook over a top mounted canister stove that is incredibly easy to use, thanks to the built-in Piezo igniter. That way no matches are needed for regular operations. However, during my first long hike with that stove, the Piezo igniter broke after two days, when I was in the middle of a large wilderness area. The igniter had probably become overheated and slightly bent out of shape. That is when my backup box of matches saved me for the remaining ten days. I remember carefully counting the number of matches and comparing that with the number of meals/ignitions remaining. There were enough matches, so did not have to split some of them down the middle with my knife to make them last longer.

If you plan to build fires, a cheap cigarette lighter often works better than matches, as you can hold the flame longer under damp kindling than a match lasts, in order to ignite the kindling. However, the flame from the lighter is very sensitive to wind, and gas consumption is not easy to calculate. I always bring a gas lighter as well. They do not weigh much. I keep it in a plastic bag with my toilet paper. I always burn the toilet paper unless there is danger of forest fires and/or you have to pack the paper out.

Various fire making tools have become popular in recent years. They are modern versions of flint and steel, where you generate sparks by scraping. The sparks then have to land in something that will readily take fire. This something usually has to be taken along; tinder, dry wood chips or cotton balls drenched in a flammable substance.

Many people like the fact that these fire steels have an almost eternal life and work as well wet as dry. At least, they function for as long as you have something dry and flammable that the sparks can ignite. My major objection to these is that it takes a bit of practice to make them work, particularly in wet and windy conditions, and that most of us need to carry something flammable along to make the fire steel serve the same purpose as a wooden match: create sparks by scraping and wood to give a brief and transferable flame. The truth is that a good fire-maker can make do with very little and a poor fire-maker is not helped by any amount or type of gear. You need to know what you can or cannot do and pick whatever gear suits you.

My own fire starting kit consists of wooden matches in water-proof wrapping, a forefinger-sized stump of a candle and a couple of small birthday candles of the trick kind that ignites anew if you try to blow them out. The whole kit weighs about 60 grams (2 oz). Many people get by with less, but the weight difference is mostly of academic interest in my opinion. As long as I have my 343 under control, I do not fuss over saving grams on small gear.

There is more to be found on the subject of fires under the chapter *Cooking*.

Long underwear

For photos and updates, see
the live part of this book at
www.smarterbackpacking.com

You can manage without underwear during the summer, even high up and far north. Yet, a pair of thin and light synthetic long johns can be very useful. It could be a pair of leggings from the ladies' wardrobe or some really thin long johns from the sports shop.

When I say long underwear I mean some kind of base layer for my legs. The overall discussion on base layers can be found in the chapters Clothing and Undershirt. The main point in regards to long underwear is that our legs are less sensitive and require less attention when we dress, than our torso.

During the summer you can manage without long underwear even in fairly damp and cool mountains. If you are hiking in warmer conditions you do not need to worry at all. My regular pants together with my rain pants usually keep me warm enough anyway.

Other considerations, however, will influence my

decision when it comes to long johns. One of them is that I prefer to have full coverage of my legs while sleeping. In fact, to protect my sleeping bag and be able to skip any form of liner, I normally sleep in socks, long underwear and a long-sleeved undershirt with a hood.

You can sleep in your hiking pants, and I often do when the weather is chilly, in combination with long johns. But you cannot be certain that the hiking pants are always dry or clean. After a wet and muddy day on the trail these pants are not something I willingly bring into my sleeping bag. On such a night, while cooking, I try to clean my pants and also try to dry them out before I get into my sleeping bag. I do this by wearing my pants on top of my long johns. This enables me to use my body heat to dry my damp pants, while I avoid having the wet fabric in direct contact with my skin, which often is chilling. On a night like that I normally leave the dry or semi-dry pants outside the sleeping bag.

For three seasons, when I am not wearing the long johns all day, I consider synthetic materials as good as merino wool. I usually pick the lightest and thinnest long johns I can find. This means I choose so-called leggings that ladies sometimes wear as stockings. Leggings basically are a pair of pantyhose without the part covering your foot. 50-60 or 80 denier leggings are usually thick enough, and they should not contain cotton. Leggings are very elastic, so if you choose the largest sizes, there is plenty of room for a guy to get into them. Nowadays you do not have to pretend that you are buying them for your female partner, as the sales assistants in ladies' lingerie shops are used to men with special tastes.

You can save 200-300 grams (6-11 oz) by choosing very light long underwear or doing without them altogether.

Map

For photos and updates, see the live part of this book at **www.smarterbackpacking.com**

Some people may claim that a digital map in a GPS-receiver weighs nothing. In my opinion, the GPS technology is not yet reliable enough for me to leave the ordinary map at home. Furthermore, an advanced GPS weighs more than a simple one and more than several paper maps. Maps do not weigh much, but if you carry several maps it may be worthwhile to cut away the parts of the maps you will not be using.

When you hike along a well marked trail you can get by without a map, at least in theory. Or, you may manage with a map that is not very detailed. But the weight of one single map is not that discouraging, if you balance it against the security of knowing where you are, or knowing how to get back to where you are supposed to be. I also like to add in the pleasure of knowing the names of some distant peaks or valleys along the path.

Yes, a digital map in your GPS does not weigh anything, but you are dependent on batteries and/or chargers, and in my world a paper map is still more foolproof.

If you hike long distances, the combined weight of the maps you carry may amount to quite a bit. So, I always cut away the parts of the maps I do not count on needing. This saves some weight and also makes the maps somewhat easier to use.

There are always areas on the map that you definitely will not walk through. Some of these areas are even impossible to access, such as the other side of a large lake or river that you would not be able to cross even if you wanted. I always make sure to keep parts of the maps showing routes to cabins, farms or small communities that I may need to visit if I have to bail out earlier or by an unplanned route. So far I have not cut away anything that later turned out to be needed.

Maps are fairly vulnerable to water and are often exposed to rain. I usually treat my maps with some of the water-proofing products you can buy for this purpose. I prefer water-based repellents for environmental reasons. They will not make the map completely waterproof and impregnable, but the protection will last a week or so. If you are going to use a certain map many times, you need to cover it with plastic film.

Medical care

For photos and updates, see
the live part of this book at
www.smarterbackpacking.com

My approach is that I cannot bring medical supplies that cover every imaginable situation. In addition, even if I had lots of medical equipment, I would not be capable of using it. What I need is basics – a way to stop lethal bleedings, something to protect small wounds, some pain killer and a way to tape sprains and damaged joints.

As with repair gear, it would not be particularly difficult to end up carrying a lot of medical supplies, especially, if you start coming down the hypochondria trail thinking of everything that could go wrong with your health on a hike. You can buy complete medical kits in sturdy, red cases that cater to every imaginable need.

Well, for starters, I skip the red case; a plastic bag does just as well and is a lot lighter. Next on my list, I examine my own competence as a medical officer. People with medical training might be able to use lots of stuff out in the field. If you are a healthcare professional, you will probably have a pretty sound evaluation of what is likely to happen, what gear can be used and what can be left at home.

But I am not one of them. For me, medical equipment for backpacking is about being able to handle small injuries myself and being able to survive bigger injuries long enough to get to professional care. Only on extremely rare occasions do people get seriously hurt in connection with backpacking. In fact, it is so unusual that it gets media attention when it happens. This, in turn, makes the media consumers believe that serious injuries are common among hikers.

Having a light pack decreases the risk of injuries more than it increases them. Sprains and other foot and leg related injuries should be rather uncommon with packs weighing less than 10 kilos (22 lbs). Stress injuries of bones, ligaments and muscles are also less common with light loads, compared to when more or less untrained office dwellers, like yours truly, heave 20 kilo (44 lbs) packs on our backs and start hiking 20 kilometers (12 miles) a day.

Knowledge is an important ingredient in medical care and cannot be replaced by gear. I recommend for everyone to go through a basic first aid course in order to know what to do and what not to do.

The basics of first aid are respiration, bleeding and chock, and they have to be addressed in that order. Lack of respiration is usually dealt with by mouth-to-mouth resuscitation, which needs no gear but some knowledge. The remaining conditions to treat are bleeding and chock.

I want to bring something with me that will stop me

or my hiking buddy to bleed to death rapidly, in case of a major injury. For this purpose I carry a small package of blood stopper – gauze and compresses that can be tied onto a major wound. This piece of equipment is a remnant from my army days and is probably overkill. I have never used it during the 30-odd years I have been carrying it, and I hope I never will. But the blood stopper only weighs 40 grams (1,5 oz) and is available quickly and easily, instead of me having to rig a blood stopper from spare clothing and duct tape. Having said this, I hope you readers understand that you can skip this piece of gear and improvise. A gaping wound can be pulled together with sports tape or duct tape until you reach the hospital. A rock or a piece of wood wrapped in a piece of cloth can be used to put pressure on arterial bleeding, and so on.

Part of a chock, should that occur, may often be caused by pain from more severe injuries, so pain killer comes in handy here. Rest, warmth and liquid are good remedies.

The remainder of my medical equipment looks like this: 3-4 band aids for smaller injuries and scratches. Half a dozen ordinary pain killers for head aches and the like; the active ingredient is less important unless you know your body reacts negatively to certain substances. Sometimes I bring a few stronger pain killers, courtesy of my doctor, but I have never used them. I also bring a couple of yards of non-elastic sports tape for stabilizing sprained ankles and similar injuries. This tape, as well as the yards of duct tape that I bring, can also be used for repairs. The repair kit, in turn, can be used for medical purposes.

You can save quite a bit of weight by not bringing too much medical equipment, and most importantly, by not bringing stuff you do not know how to use anyway. I focus on what I need to survive until I can get to a hospital.

Miscellaneous

For photos and updates, see
the live part of this book at
www.smarterbackpacking.com

*Here I share details about a few odds and ends that
can be found in my pack, but do not really deserve
a chapter of their own.*

COMB. A comb is not really a necessary piece of gear,
but most people will probably bring one anyway. Unless
you have lots of hair to manage (my own managerial
duties are receding), a short, plastic comb, preferably in
a clearly visible color in case you should drop it, does not
weigh more than 5-10 grams (1/5-2/5 oz).

WRITING MATERIAL. When on the trail, I write a sort
of diary, as background material for books and web
pages, but also in order to have something to read back
at the old folks home some day when my legs might no
longer carry me towards the horizons. I use something
as superbly low-tech as an ordinary wooden pencil.
Usually I only bring a piece that is 70-100 mm (3-4
inches). I easily sharpen it with my knife and it works in
most circumstances where the space-age technology
deserts me. My paper is ordinary A4/letter size that I

fold four times. This gives me 16 small rectangles to write on. Being small, they drive me to write with very small print. I put a number on each rectangle, as they will not be in sequence when the paper is unfolded.

Three-four sheets is enough for a week. Writing materials are of course a highly personal matter. Plastic paper materials withstand just about anything, but I do not feel the need to acquire that. Papers and pencil are always protected well enough in a plastic Ziploc bag that goes inside my pack.

Sometimes I may need or want paper and pencil more readily available, for instance, when I want to navigate by jotting down exact times when I left specific locations. Then the plastic bag goes in one of the pouches on my waist belt or shoulder straps, together with map, compass, GPS and camera.

WHISTLE. I always bring it and have never needed it. I hope this will continue, but should I need to call for help at any time, I know that my vocal cords are transient but the whistle is eternal. It stays in a pocket in my pants, attached with a cord to keep it there until needed.

MONEY AND TICKETS. I usually bring a couple of credit cards, ID and some paper money as well as airline tickets, in a plastic bag. When possible, I use electronic airline tickets. Car keys usually end up in the same bag.

SUNSCREEN. The most important sun protection is the clothing, which is easy to forget. Using thin and light clothing as I do makes it more comfortable to wear them even when the weather is really hot.

Bringing a large bottle of sunscreen that is not needed is not good weight economy. I try to pick a high protection factor and small containers, but in some parts of the world it is not easy to calculate how much will be needed during a given time period, maybe none. It all depends on the weather and your skin type. I remember a 10-day hike in an unexpected heat wave, in which I burnt myself after running out of sunscreen. Though, I did not fare as badly as I did during a snowshoe trip in the Colorado Rockies, a long time ago. After that trip, my face looked like a scalded tomato, and my skin came off in long strips. However, I usually manage with about 50 grams (2 oz) for a week-long trip.

BEARBAGGING. In northern Europe you do not have to worry about bears stealing your food, although there are plenty of bears. Maybe the problem will increase, maybe not. I often cook in my tent and store all my food in the tent. For other parts of the world, particulary North America, special care is needed, especially in places where there are lots of hikers and bear have become habituated to them. Some techniques for keeping food safe is shown on the website that is part of this book.

.

Mobile phone

For photos and updates, see
the live part of this book at
www.smarterbackpacking.com

The mobile phone is in my opinion more a question of comfort than of safety when you are backpacking. But it does not weigh much and it easily defends its place in the pack unless you are an extreme minimalist.

The jury is still out on the need for bringing a mobile phone while backpacking when it comes to areas where the coverage is sketchy. If you are hiking in an area with good coverage this is obviously a no brainer, but areas frequented by hikers usually have poor coverage simply because there is not enough people and traffic to motivate the phone companies to invest.

This means that bringing a phone because you want to be able to call for help in an emergency is at best chancy. Satellite phones are better for this purpose, but more expensive and heavier. I have backpacked alone for decades before there were any mobile phones and so, I am probably less scared of not being able to call for help than many others.

In any event I do think that a mobile phone is good to bring in my pack, out of comfort. There is often mobile coverage at trail heads, where you start and end your hike. However, pay phones are getting more and more scarce, particularly in small communities bordering on wilderness areas. So, you cannot rely on finding a phone booth to tell family and friends that you are back on the grid and safe. For this reason the mobile phone justifies its existence in my pack.

If I can speculate, I would think that the mobile phone in a few years will also contain a camera with features so much better than most have today, and that it will serve the average photographer on the trail very well. The same goes for GPS functions. So the mobile phone might in a short while make two chapters in this book obsolete, but the website will be kept updated ."

Most mobile phones weigh around 100 grams (3-4 oz), unless you pick a more sophisticated model that only has telephone calls as a hobby. But you can save around 100 grams (3-4 oz) by picking a light one instead of one of the heavier ones on the market. For most of us who go on moderate hikes, there is no need to bring a charger, if you load the phone fully before you leave and use it sparingly.

Pants

For photos and updates, see
the live part of this book at
www.smarterbackpacking.com

Thin, light and strong pants are readily available if you turn away from the mainstream style of hiking and outdoor pants. Light pants for runners are insect-proof and dry quickly. They do not weigh much or take up much space in the pack when the weather makes you more inclined to wear shorts. When you wear thin pants, you can deal with even the worst kind of weather if you add long johns and/or rain pants.

I have come to the conclusion that I can do much better without specially designed pants, than I used to believe. And the fabric does not have to be as rugged as it was in my old pants. For many years I used second-hand military pants while hiking. Some, made out of wool, weighed around a kilo (2 lbs) or more – great for hikes in the late fall, but heavy. Nowadays I use light synthetic pants more akin to runners' pants than to hikers' pants.

Modern synthetic fabrics are incredibly strong, and my opinion is that they do not need any reinforcements on knees or seat, for ordinary use. I might be a bit dull, but just as I do not really understand why I should wear rain garments when it is not raining, I do not understand why my pants should be patched before they have been worn through.

By ordinary use I mean that you do not slide down rock-faces on your bum or spend a lot of time on your knees, which is something climbers or cavers might do. But I know of people that have slipped down rocky slopes in pants literally made out of the same ripstop used for sleeping bags, without any holes to show for it. This is not a recommendation, only an example of the fact that many kinds of extremely strong and light synthetic fabrics are available today.

Right now I am using a pair of thin, home-made synthetic pants that weigh 160 grams (5.5 oz). In spite of fairly frequent use during four hiking seasons, they do not show any wear, neither at the bottom nor on the knees. On my latest long hike, the thread used at the bottom of the legs was worn out and the seam was unfolding. The fabric being undamaged, I just fixed the seam with some dental floss. After returning home I brought out my sewing machine and used new thread to rejuvenate the seams around both pant legs. Now they are as good as new.

I find that the advantages with light pants like these are so many that it would take a lot for me to switch back to something heavier and more "rugged" on my hikes. The light pants are definitely strong enough. They are bug proof, they are windproof, they are cool, and last but not least, they dry out really quickly.

The advantage of quick-drying pants can hardly be stressed enough. Nowadays I need not worry one little bit if my pants get wet while crossing creeks, or during brief rain showers. I just walk straight across creeks or rivers that come my way, without changing pants, shoes or socks (for more details check those chapters). Pants that are wet to my knees are usually almost dry after twenty minutes of hiking, bar half an inch or so at the very bottom. And this is true even in a cool and damp climate such as the Scandinavian mountains. In a warm and dry inland climate you can literally see the damp receding and after five minutes you kind of miss the cool feeling.

If my pants are damp or wet when I set up camp at night, I pull on my long johns first, then a warm jacket on my torso and finally the damp pants on top. They will usually turn completely dry from my body heat, without direct contact with my skin, while I am cooking and eating. If they are not completely dry then, they will be, the next morning, when I pull them on just before I start hiking again.

Something I used to like about military garments was the multitude of spacious pockets. I had plenty of room for knives, compasses, tape, gloves and so on. Nowadays I take so little gear along that I do not need any pockets at all on my pants. And because I do not have many pockets, I have discovered that knives, compasses, maps, cups and gloves are things that I do not need to carry in my pockets.

In situations where I need to carry a map and compass, I usually carry my pack, and then the map and compass rest in a pocket on my waist belt. The knife I almost only use in connection with cooking and camp life and it is then handy in the pack beside me.

Carrying things in thigh pockets is less energy-efficient than carrying them on your back. For the same reason, heavy shoes (see the chapter on Shoes) are more strenuous to carry on your feet than on your back, because, due to leverage and biomechanical reasons, you are forced to lift them vertically against gravity even when you are moving horizontally.

Since I like to hike long distances, from early to late, I am seldom far away from my pack. The longest distance normally is when I am reducing the surplus from my alimentary tract. For hikers who are fishermen or have other interests, spacious pockets may be more important. It is up to everyone to analyze his or her specific needs and choose gear accordingly. The only item I habitually carry in my pant pocket is a whistle, and sometimes damp gloves that dry out very well in what I call "groin pockets", that is the ordinary front pockets on most pants that open at your hip and slant towards the groin.

Some types of pants weigh less than 100 grams (3.5 oz) and are still remarkably strong. Ordinary hiking pants often weigh around 400-500 grams (1 lb). Shaving weight off things you wear on your body may seem unnecessary, but thin fabrics also has other advantages. And logically, you have to move your pants from point A to point B with your muscles. The lighter they, and everything else, are, the easier this is. This truth is really brought home to hikers when the weather gets hot and you want to wear shorts. When your pants get folded up and put in the pack you really appreciate that they are light.

For experienced hikers, as well as for beginners, psychological factors are the main reasons that make people hesitate to turn their back on the just-about bombproof, Kevlar-reinforced super pants! But many ounces and sometimes a pound can be saved, and my experience so far is that light-weight pants only have positive effects all around.

Pillow

For photos and updates, see
the live part of this book at
www.smarterbackpacking.com

*Hikers often make pillows by putting extra gear into
stuff sacks. But if you are into light packing with
very little extra gear, this is not so easy. Also, pillows
are a personal matter. Some people do better
without them, while others cannot sleep without
something under their ear. If this is true for you, you
can find inflatable pillows that are very light.*

The need for having something under your head when
you sleep varies among people. If you sleep well without
a pillow, you can skip the pillow along with this chapter.
As for me, I sleep on my side and need something quite
substantial tucked between my shoulder and my ear, in
order to sleep peacefully.

You can often create a makeshift pillow by putting
some extra clothing into a stuff sack and tie a knot on it.
But for lightweight backpackers that is a problem
because you seldom have any spare clothing. Fairly often,
I am wearing almost every single piece of clothing when
I am in my sleeping bag. Other pieces of clothing such as

rain gear might already be in use, reinforcing thin or short sleeping pads. This is the great (and maybe only weak) aspect of carrying a light load; you have a lack of pillow stuffing.

One solution is to use some of your food for building volume, and then adding some buffering in order to not have the noodles crunching in your ear all night. But the last couple of days of a hike you do not have much food either.

So in recent years, which coincides with advancing age for yours truly, I have started bringing with me pillows of different varieties. One model I have used is a very light, inflatable Tyvek pillow. These are available at least in the United States. They weigh 20-30 grams (3/4-1 oz) and are comfortable, but a bit too big to fit inside the hood of my sleeping bag. I prefer the pillow inside the sleeping bag. It is much easier to adjust, particularly when the hood is cinched up against the cold.

The main disadvantages with these pillows are that they puncture easily and that the valve tends to leak. Of course, you can inflate them five times every night if you have to, but I would rather sleep.

The best solution so far has turned out to be an inflatable plastic bag that comes with a 3 litres (3 quarts) of bag-in-box wine. This bag can also be used as an extra water container when you have to carry large amounts of water.

Some people bring tailor-made pillows made from perforated foam, which makes them very light, in water-proof pillow cases.

You can save 20-100 grams (¾-3 oz) by either skipping the pillow or choose a light variety.

Poles

For photos and updates, see
the live part of this book at
www.smarterbackpacking.com

Hiking poles can be found in different materials and different weights. If you use them as tent poles, you should use poles that are a bit rugged. Telescopic poles are convenient, but do weigh a bit more.

In the last decades, the attitude towards hikers with poles has changed, from being looked upon as "someone who has lost his/her skis" to a tool used by most hikers. Sometimes I wonder why it took hikers so long to go from one walking staff, which has been common for thousands of years, to using poles. I have always used one staff while hiking but would now never go without my two trusty poles.

Apart from all the advantages of hiking poles, the most important from a weight-saving point of view is that they can be used as tent or tarp poles. This also makes them difficult to do without, at least if you move about in tundra areas without trees as much as I do.

The heavier poles on the market weigh around 500 grams (18 oz) a pair, and they are often telescopic poles made out of some kind of aluminum alloy. The lightest poles weigh around 200 grams (6-7 oz) and are fixed lengths of carbon fiber.

If you use the poles for your tent or tarp, and you like to vary the height and angling of your shelter, like I do, telescopic poles are almost the only choice. They are also easier to transport going to and from your hike, when strapped to the pack in short mode.

My own choice is telescopic poles in two sections, made of a quite durable material, weighing around 450 grams (16 oz) a pair. They are a bit on the heavy side. On my trips, I've broken a couple of poles, both the heavier kind and light carbon fiber poles. This has made me a bit conservative concerning weight and durability. Losing a tent pole by falling on it on a scree slope, in the middle of a treeless wilderness, is not so fun. I have done that and was lucky to be able to patch it to a fixed length that was not too short for my tent.

You can save a bit of weight by choosing the lighter poles on the market. If you use them as tent poles, this saves weight overall. But if you are going where it is difficult to replace broken poles, don't choose the lightest type.

Rain

For photos and updates, see
the live part of this book at
www.smarterbackpacking.com

During continuous rain everything becomes wet, sooner or later. Or, almost everything. The sleeping bag has to be kept dry at all costs. Rain can cause hypothermia and it is important that you know how this dangerous, downward spiral may affect you, so that you can counter it with clothing, food and drink. When you learn how to hike in rain you become liberated – free to enjoy your hike in spite of the weather.

This is a chapter on rain in general. Other chapters deal with specific gear for rain.

Rain is in many ways troublesome for a hiker, particularly if it goes on and on. In the long run, after several days of rain, most of your gear will be wet or at least damp. And with damp clothing you can easily become hypothermic. What begins with general discomfort can become apathy and extreme discomfort. You can in fact freeze to death, even if the temperature is above freezing. But this outcome is of course extreme.

More common is that you are cold and you feel the vacation is a total failure.

In my Scandinavian mountains, rain is always to be expected. It is not common that the rain pours down day after day, but it could happen. Frequent showers and persistent drizzle in the company of a cold wind are more common. If you are hiking in these circumstances, you should learn to cope with rain so that your hike does not turn into a complete disaster.

Even with perfect rain gear, you can count on becoming a bit damp if the rain continues for a while. It cannot be stressed enough how important it is to keep your sleeping bag dry in those circumstances. You can read more about this in the chapter Stuff sacks. It is also important that you are equipped with clothes that dry quickly and provide some protection against hypothermia, even when they are wet. This means that cotton in any shape or form is something you must scrupulously avoid – no T-shirts or bandannas in the material; not even fabrics with a cotton and synthetic mixture. I have found that there are many 100% synthetic materials that are just as comfortable, as well as thinner and lighter. Thin fabrics always dry faster than the same fabric in thicker versions.

Thin, synthetic shirts and pants is what I use and recommend. There is one exception. Thin merino wool base layers do not dry as fast as synthetics but are in my opinion more comfortable to wear when damp or wet. You can read more about this in the chapters Undershirt and Clothing.

Strenuous exercise, like hiking, often makes you damp underneath your more or less breathable rain gear. This is definitely to prefer to becoming wet from large amounts of much colder water from the outside, but the dampness of your own sweat still has a chilling effect. As long as you are in motion, this is often not much of a problem, at least not if the weather is not too cold and windy. But the moment you come to a halt, you tend to become chilled. To counter this, it is important, especially in rainy weather, to put on something insulating for short or long breaks.

Putting on more clothes at break is not always as easy to do as it is to say. If you are chilled even while hiking and weary when you sit down, you may easily want to skip the hassle with extra clothing. Struggling to open your pack in pouring rain does not feel so great. Also, you must keep your insulating clothing dry, which usually means you have to take off your rain jacket, don the insulating garment and then put your rain jacket back on top of it.

A dangerous, downward spiral of hypothermia can begin like that. It is a slippery slope of increasing apathy that can start with you becoming chilled while you are hiking. Being cold makes it awkward and uncomfortable to pause, so you skip these. This apathy also leads to skipping regular handfuls of snacks being popped into your mouth. Because you cannot lounge in the grass and the sun, you might skip lunch. You just walk. Everything becomes heavy, grey and wet. Finally, you are so tired that you have to stop. You just sit down; collapse into a big heap and wish you were somewhere else. Whose idea was it to go on this hike?

If the above sounds like I have been there it is because I have been there. In a situation like that it is paramount that you restore your body heat by putting on warm clothes as well as providing your body with calories to fuel your inner furnace. It is also essential that you are on guard and aware of what is happening to you, or to someone in your hiking group. Unless it is winter, you seldom run the risk to end up in a life-threatening condition, only the risk of feeling totally miserable. But this was hardly the vision you had when you planned your hike.

In winter, the margins of error are smaller and the distance between being tired and apathetic is shorter. It happens that people freeze to death in the mountains beside packs full of warm clothing and food, which they were too tired to access and use.

Good rain gear, awareness of the hypothermia danger and easy access to a big bag of snacks are important tools for you to be able to enjoy hiking even when it is raining. If you are warm and your stomach is full, you are certainly able to enjoy seeing a curtain of rain, topped with a rainbow, rushing across the valley to meet you. Few things lull me to sleep better than resting in my dry and warm sleeping bag, listening to the rain pattering on the fly of my shelter.

Rain cover

For photos and updates, see
the live part of this book at
www.smarterbackpacking.com

Every backpack I have ever used has leaked after a while when I have been hiking in rain. This includes occasions when I have had separate rain covers over my pack. Nowadays, I leave the rain cover at home and simply use water-proof bags to protect the essentials in my pack.

Most packs are made of thick, coated fabrics which may appear waterproof for the inexperienced hiker. They very seldom are. All packs I have ever used have leaked, even after fairly short periods of rain; at least after the pack has been used a year or two. In recent years, packs that are claimed to be waterproof have been introduced. The future will show if this holds true and if there is a market for them. Personally, I take no interest in them, because most of the gear in my pack does not get damaged by being wet; and because there are better and more bombproof ways to protect the stuff that has to be kept dry at all costs. You will need to do this anyway, as stuffing wet gear into a waterproof pack tends to wet the dry stuff already in there.

A rain cover for the backpack is a common piece of gear to keep the rain out of the pack. Rain covers usually consist of a large piece of waterproof cloth that is strapped to the outside of the pack like a huge swimming cap. I do not use these covers, since they in fact do not keep the gear inside the pack dry. The reason is that the cover leaves the entire back of the pack, where the shoulder straps and waist belt attach, uncovered. The rain will run down the shoulders and back of the hiker and permeate seams and fabric, entering the pack in that way.

In my humble opinion, a rain cover that does not stop water from entering my pack is a completely useless piece of gear. There is one method that keeps parts of the outside of the pack reasonably dry in rain, and that is using an umbrella. The umbrella also protects the back of the pack from getting wet and soaking your dry clothes. More details about this can be found in the Umbrella chapter. You can also find information on my choices in the chapters Rain and Dry sacks.

I do not see it as a big problem that packs leak, as long as I do not expect them not to. Likewise, I do not feel that it is worth the trouble trying to waterproof them. Some people have in fact accepted the consequences of leaking packs and made packs completely out of mesh. The main function of a pack is to carry your equipment. Protection from wear and water are secondary functions and can be more or less discarded.

It suffices to say that most gear can handle water very

well. Food is usually packed in waterproof bags anyway and the same is the case with medical equipment. Knives, spoons, cups, stove, sleeping pads and so on can handle being wet very well. What has to be kept dry at all costs is the sleeping bag and your change of clothes. These are much easier to protect separately, than by trying to make the whole pack waterproof.

My way of keeping items dry is using separate and truly waterproof stuff sacks. So I skip the rain cover and that way I save weight. Depending on how large the rain cover is and how sturdy the fabric is, the weight saving can be substantial. Commercial-use rain covers range from 75 grams (2.5 oz) to 300 grams (11 oz).

Rain jacket

For photos and updates, see
the live part of this book at
www.smarterbackpacking.com

Luckily, good quality rain jackets are easy to find on the market. Often, it is better to bring one of those on your hike and leave heavier shells at home. I find it more comfortable to use my rain jacket as seldom as possible, in order to minimize condensation problems. As a consequence, I only use my rain jacket when it is raining heavily.

Many heavy rain jackets can be found on the market. You can fairly easily save around 500 grams (18 oz) by choosing one of the lighter ones instead of a heavier one. I consider the majority of the so-called shell jackets heavy. They are common in many wardrobes today and are usually made of some kind of Mextex. In my opinion, most of them are unnecessarily heavy and thick for hiking. Most of them are in fact made not for hiking, but for waiting at the bus stop, albeit with a wilderness look that might be confusing. Even if the marketing information claims that they have been used on Mount

Everest, I prefer to leave them at home.

These heavy jackets are excellent in town or for other kinds of outdoor activities, when I am not as physically active as when I am hiking, and I have blessed them many times on outings with my kids – and when at the bus stop.

However, for hiking I do not like to wear garments that, in fact, breathe as little as they do, unless I absolutely have to, which is when it is raining so much so that my umbrella does not give sufficient protection.

This is how I dress when I hike: As long as it is not so rainy or windy that my windshirt and umbrella do not keep my dry, my rain jacket rests in my pack. And then it is very nice that the jacket weighs 200 grams (7 oz) and not 750 grams (27 oz). But when the weather gets really nasty, with low temperatures, high winds and horizontal rain, the rain jacket, with its main function to keep the torso dry, is very important from a safety point of view. Hypothermia can kill even if temperatures are above freezing.

The combination of a light windshirt of 100-150 grams (3-5 oz) and a light rain jacket of 200-300 grams (7-11 oz) is actually lighter than many shell jackets, and infinitely more adaptable to different kinds of weather and different levels of exertion. Not uncommonly, the combination is also less expensive than some of the flagship shells from well-known brands.

If you only use the rain jacket when the weather is truly miserable, it does not have to be as rugged, as you will use it fairly seldom. That way, even a light, thin rain jacket will last many years. A rip is easily fixed with a piece of duct tape and that patch can last for years if you are not particularly sensitive to how it looks – and you do not have to be, if you only use it when the weather is extremely poor.

If you spend much of your outings in base camps, perhaps using fires a lot, you may feel that the lightest rain jackets are not rugged enough. They are more vulnerable to sparks from the fire than the heavier garments. This could be a reason to choose a slightly heavier jacket. But you can also choose another garment as general shell when it is not raining. As for me, I always use my windshirt as shell in those kinds of situations. The jacket is less expensive and does not have to be waterproof.

When using so-called waterproof/breathable garments it is important to remember that they are much more waterproof than they are breathable. Most of the moisture is in fact not transported through the fabric, but ventilated through different openings. This means that you should always have the jacket as open as circumstances allow, if you want to minimize condensation inside the garment. This is also a good idea in tents: If it is not raining, you do not have to close the foretent). So, do not tighten the jacket around the wrists or the throat if that can be avoided. And leave the front zipper as unzipped as possible.

You can save quite a bit of weight by choosing a light rain jacket instead of a heavy one. Put the jacket you probably already have on a scale, and then ponder if it is worth its weight. My experience is that the heavy-expedition weight rain jacket is more useful in the bus line (or on winter ski trips) but for three season hikes, a lighter and cheaper jacket is better. But, it must be a rain jacket by definition. It cannot be so light and cheap that it doesn't keep out the rain.

Rain pants

For photos and updates, see the live part of this book at **www.smarterbackpacking.com**

A pair of light rain pants need not be expensive. Like the rain jacket, rain pants are important for comfort and safety in colder climates and/or high elevation trails. When the wind blows cold, the rain pants also keep you warm, which means you sometimes can leave the long johns at home. Chaps are a variety of pants that ventilate better and are more flexible on some occasions.

Some hikers simply skip the rain pants and keep warm by constant and vigorous motion. This probably works well in the summertime, in protected areas like the Appalachian Trail, if you are fit and strong. I would not recommend it for tundra areas like northern Alaska, not even in summertime. However, you can save a considerable amount of weight by choosing from the lightest rain pants on the market.

My own favorite solution for leggings in rough weather is thin, synthetic pants coupled with light rain pants on top. The rain pants should weigh at the most

200-300 grams (7-11 oz). You can even find rain pants that weigh in at half of that. I have never needed rain pants with side zips. They can be useful if you use boots that are a nuisance to lace off and on, but you pay a penalty in weight and complexity. Since I use light running shoes that are easily taken on and off, I don't need zips like that at all.

In summer weather you could consider your rain pants as something to not only keep you dry, but also keep you warm. Leave the long johns at home and put on the rain pants when it is cold and windy.

In theory, a pair of shell pants in waterproof/ breathable material could be used as both standard pants and rain pants. All in one, that is. Personally, I am sceptical, for the same reason that I describe elsewhere: I do not like to dress in rain clothing unless it is raining. Even the best waterproof/ breathables are a whole lot more waterproof than breathable. They tend to collect condensation if you walk in them for some time while carrying a pack. If you are mostly standing still, that's a different ballgame, but in this book we are mostly concerned with hiking.

All-round pants also tend to be on the heavy side, which is not so comfortable, and there is always a risk that daily wear-and-tear could make them leak sooner or later.

My particular favorite, as far as rain pants go, is a combination of chaps and home-made rain shorts. This is a good combination of protection from rain and ventilation. The chaps will reach up to mid-thigh, and used together with an umbrella they give adequate protection in most types of rain. In really hard and windblown rain I fold up my umbrella and put on a pair of rain shorts for complete protection. Rain shorts are as far as I know not commercially available at the time when I am writing this, but sometimes you can find kilts or skirts made of waterproof material that serve the same purpose, more or less.

In any event, you can pretty easily buy two pairs of inexpensive and light rain pants and cut off the legs at mid thigh on both of them. Of course you cut the shorts so that they overlap the chaps by 10-15 centimeters (4-6 inches). You can also use only one pair of pants and instead tack on 10-15 centimeters at the bottom of each leg, to create a similar overlap. For the addition to the legs you can use really light and waterproof material, like silnylon, since the breathability of the fabric is of little importance at the bottom of the legs, as condensation is ventilated, not breathed, in that area.

Picking a pair of really light rain pants can save 100-300 grams (3-10 oz), compared to choosing the heavier ones.

Repairs

For photos and updates, see
the live part of this book at
www.smarterbackpacking.com

*Being prepared for everything is a tempting idea,
but most of what goes into a lightweight pack can
be repaired, or at least kept serviceable, without
much gear. In order to keep on hiking, one has to
focus on function, not on beauty. Some dental floss
and duct tape goes a long way, and lots of weight
can be saved by staying away from multi tools.*

You have to be able to fix some gear in case it would
break, in order to not put your whole hike at risk. My
repair gear consists of a few yards of duct tape rolled
around an old plastic film can from the days of silver
bromide. The can contains half a yard of dental floss
threaded on a suitable sewing needle, four or five safety
pins, a couple of leather/fabric rivets and a yard or two
of thin and pliable wire.

Most of my hiking gear is made of fabric and almost
everything made of fabric can be made serviceable with
the help of a few safety pins, some thread and some
pieces of duct tape.

The duct tape can be used as band aids or sports tape for injuries and the tape that is part of the medical gear can also be used for repairs. I once patched a tent that had been split from top to bottom by a bear, using sports tape.

A safety pin is another nifty product that can rapidly repair lots of broken gear. Wire is very strong, withstands a great deal of abrasion and heat and can be used for mending everything from hiking poles to cooking utensils.

If you want to be prepared for everything that could (im)possibly happen, your repair kit could become very heavy, particularly if you bring a hefty multi tool which may weigh 150-300 grams (5-10 oz). But most of the time you will have little use for all the tools they contain and often you lighten your load if you replace the multi tool with separate tools. A small pair of scissors, a small pair of tweezers and a small knife usually weighs less and works better than a complete multi tool filled with screwdrivers that can fix nothing on your gear. Nowadays, I carry a small Swiss Army knife that only contains what I really need and can use. You can certainly also find small, non-Swiss-Army multi knives that work. Just check the weight and examine what tools they contain.

Many experienced hikers have started their hiking careers with their pack filled with repair gear and found that they were never used. Yet, bringing them has become a habit, and you are of course not supposed to use them every time. I went hiking during several decades without even considering doing something about my repair stuff. The inexperienced hiker is always tempted to be "always prepared" which is a good thing if we talk about state of mind, but not when we talk about gear. With a bit of critical thinking, both groups can save quite a bit in the repair department. I speak from experience.

Shelter

For photos and updates, see the live part of this book at **www.smarterbackpacking.com**

Roof over your head is one of the three big and bulky lumps of the pack. This is a complex area with many pros and cons, but well worth considering because of the weight involved. In this chapter I try to make a long story short without being embarrassingly sparse with words.

The shelter is important for safety as well as for feeling safe; for psychological reasons. Choosing a lighter shelter is therefore a challenge for both experienced and inexperienced backpackers. But the gain can be counted in kilos (several lbs) so it is well worth it to ponder whether one's attitude towards lighter shelters is based on rationality or sentiments.

The traditional mountain tent is a double-wall tent, with an inner-tent made of wind-proof but not waterproof fabric. Covering this, more or less completely, is an outer tent or a rain fly, made of waterproof fabric. A common feature is also a fore-tent – a floorless area between inner and outer tents.

Many of these mountaineering tents are very rugged and can literally handle a winter storm on the polar ice cap. This is impressive, considering that they do not weigh many kilos. The disadvantage, however, is that this over-capacity makes them unnecessarily heavy and sturdy for three-season use well away from the polar ice cap.

Among lighter alternatives we find the tarp tents. These are often very light. They are single-wall tents with floor and bug-netting and usually made of lighter fabrics as they are not made for storms on the ice cap. Tarp tents weigh less than a kilo per person and the lightest, at the time of writing (2010), weigh less than half a kilo (1 lb) for a one-person tent.

In my experience, the lightest tarp tents do well at fairly well-protected tent sites, if you take them above timberline. Below timberline you can use them without any special consideration. They are not as windproof as the traditional mountaineering tents, but this should not be of any great concern for an experienced person. I have spent more than 75 nights in tarp tents and only on one occasion did I wish for a more stable tent. Or, earplugs. The tent did not break, but was compressed by the wind, and the whip cracking of the fabric in the wind made sleep impossible. I finally had to break camp and walk about 5 kilometers (3 miles) to a small hut where I had breakfast and slept for about an hour.

Tarp tents are a good solution for the person who still wants the comfort and protection of a tent, but with less weight penalty than with traditional tents. You have a bug proof space and usually better views because you are not totally surrounded by fabric. This is nice, and it makes for better ventilation and less condensation, but there can also be a downside to better ventilation which is spelled draft. Tarp tents as well as pure tarps might create the need for a slightly warmer sleeping bag, or more clothes worn in the sleeping bag, on occasion. However, this can be difficult to calculate because less ventilation means more condensation, which will lower the insulating properties of your sleep system. In my view, less condensation is more valuable and extra down usually insulates better than the same weight of tent fabric.

Let us move on to the tarp, which in its simplest form is a rectangular piece of fabric. Most of the time they are more sophisticated, in order to give better protection against wind and precipitation. Tarps do not have floors, nor do they usually give protection from all directions. They also lack bug protection. One advantage is that you live and sleep closer to the natural world surrounding the tarp. They have superb ventilation in most instances, which also means that they can be draughty. For forest hikes when there are no bugs around, there is nothing I rather use, because of comfort, weight and pure enjoyment.

I do not consider the draughtiness of tarps and tarp tents as a major disadvantage. I do suffer more from the condensation in double-wall, traditional tents. In spite of advanced ventilation, condensation can still be a huge problem. Occasionally, everything becomes damp, including the sensitive sleeping bag that is pressed up against the inner tent, which presses against the fly and soaks up the moisture there. Both tarps and tarp tents can sometimes suffer from condensation, but I find that less of a problem because I can usually increase their ventilating properties.

Many tarps and tarp tents are not constructed for above-timberline use, except occasionally. In my Scandinavian mountains, however, you are often in Arctic conditions. You are a long way from the forest and you walk day after day in exposed areas. Extreme winds and rain above timberline put great demands on your shelter. Such extreme weather conditions do not often occur, but your shelter should have margins to handle pretty nasty weather. My experiences of both home-made tarps and tarp tents in above-timberline conditions are good, and I prefer them to traditional double-wall tents because they are more comfortable, nicer to live in and nine times out of ten they are less condensation-prone.

As the interest in lighter packs has increased, more and more tent types have become available, which are reasonably light weight and yet provide the sense of safety that many people require. For the less experienced hiker, a tent that is traditional, but reasonably light weight, is definitely a good choice. Especially when two or three people share a shelter, the weight of the shelter may represent only 1-1.5 kilo (2-3 lbs) per person. That means, the hikers still manage the "three kilos for the three big ones" or 343, if they choose a light pack and a light sleeping bag.

The experienced hiker may feel more comfortable, both practically and psychologically, when using a shelter that feels thinner and where the hiker is not enclosed on all sides by fabric.

Shorts
and such

For photos and updates, see
the live part of this book at
www.smarterbackpacking.com

*A pair of really thin and light synthetic underwear
is an excellent solution. Cotton is something I avoid
like the plague. If the underwear in design and cut
looks like a pair of cycling shorts or regular shorts
they can be used without pants on top. Light
running shorts or merino boxers also have this great
double use.*

Putting one piece of gear to several uses is a good way to
save weight. I think combining underwear and shorts is
a great advantage.

Hygiene and underwear are areas were lifetime habits
easily get in the way of rational thinking. My views on
hygiene are presented in a separate chapter that will
probably make some readers close this book forever. If
we stick to underwear here, let me begin by saying that
it is quite possible to hike without any underwear at all,
at least for men. How that would work for women I have
no first hand experience to share, but I suspect that it is

not as simple, unless you hike in a skirt.

My suggestions for women: Two pairs of really thin synthetic or silk panties, where one pair is washed every day and the other worn could be a solution. If you are hiking in a predominantly dry and warm climate even merino underwear might dry without a problem. In cooler and wetter climates my bet is on the synthetic or silk versions. Another solution is panty liners made of paper; then you do not have to wash your panties every day.

The fact is that we, humanity, have lived without special underwear for most of our existence. Underwear started out with the primary objective of protecting the other clothes, so that they would not need to be washed as frequently. This was because many clothes in the olden days were made of wool, which was difficult to wash and dry. But when I am backpacking in my thin synthetic pants, I do not have to worry much about that. Unless I am out on a long hike, my pants will not get particularly dirty from the inside, and on a long hike, the pants are usually quick to dry if I wash them when the weather is benevolent.

Now, I do not often hike without underwear because I found that they can also serve as shorts in hot weather. I found two different varieties of underwear that work very well. One is light synthetic shorts for runners. These are thin and light shorts that usually have an inner layer made of mesh. They are easy to wash and dry quickly, and while this is happening, you can hike in your pants only. A very neat solution is also to simply take off your pants when you get warm and continue hiking in these shorts/underwear.

The other short solution, which I prefer these days, is to use merino boxer shorts or cycling shorts. Merino wool is excellent for all underwear. The wool keeps them from starting to smell way longer than cotton or synthetic underwear. If you choose a boxer cut, they can be used as shorts, without being embarrassingly similar to underwear. Merino boxers for women look like any pair of cycling shorts. The ones for men usually has a fly, which tells on you, but as long as you are in less populated areas that should be of no concern. Or, you can simply sew the fly up. However, there is also true merino cycling shorts without fly and also a bit longer in the legs. Those are the ones I choose these days.

Merino underwear can be all right without laundering for a week or more, although you should probably claim you have that on hearsay only, in these hygiene-fixated times. My view on underwear is the same as for milk; if it does not smell it is all right.

If you have the chance, it is a good idea to hang up your merino underwear to ventilate for a while every day or night. But even if you have them on 24/7, they work very well and will not smell bad. Try it out at home for a couple of days if you are sceptical of only bringing one set of underwear on a hike.

Some readers will no doubt think that what I have written about underwear is pretty nauseating. In that case I recommend two thin, synthetic, or silk, pairs of underwear, no matter if they are shorts or panties. They should be as thin as possible, and you wash one pair every day. Cold water is normally quite sufficient, although soiled areas might need a bit of soap. This pair dries on your pack or inside your rain jacket, while the other pair is being used.

You can save 200-300 grams (6-10 oz) by limiting the number of underwear you bring along and by thinking multi-purpose. No need to bring one pair of hiking shorts, one pair of swimming shorts and any number of underwear. Seven pairs of cotton boxer shorts for a week's hike is not good practice if you want to lower your pack weight, and it is not at all necessary, unless you have locked you mind into thinking it is.

Sleep system

For photos and updates, see the live part of this book at **www.smarterbackpacking.com**

Down sleeping bags weighing 400-800 grams (14-38 oz) are good for temperatures around freezing. Down is still superior to any other material as far as volume, insulating capacity, longevity and weight goes. In my opinion, there are few pieces of gear that are more worthy of a substantial investment.

The sleep system belongs to the three big ones, meaning, some hefty weight savings are available here. When it comes to sleep systems, there are lots of factors to be considered. I will be very brief, maybe too brief, but a ton of information is available in books and on the Internet. Here I present only my own simple conclusions.

Sleeping gear or sleep system is a good term for what you need to maintain body temperature while taking (usually) nightly rest. Because, be aware that there are other methods to rest than using a sleeping bag. One such method is using a quilt, usually without a hood but with a foot box. As the quilt covers you only on top, and leaves insulating the underside to the sleeping pad, you can save weight, as less material is needed than for a sleeping bag.

There are also top-bags which are more like sleeping bags than quilts, where the insulation on the underside has been replaced by a long pocket where you can fit in your sleeping pad. You might also consider it a quilt with a pocket underneath.

My own experience of hiking in mountains during summer and early fall is that I need a sleep system that keeps me warm in temperatures down to around freezing point. The lightest solution to deliver this are quilts of top quality down and fabrics. Currently they weigh between 250-350 grams (9-14 oz). I have used both down and synthetic quilts and find them excellent for summer hikes. However, today I feel the quilt no longer has the weight advantage over the lightest sleeping bags, as it did in the past. But if you want the lightest they certainly are it.

Today, I can find sleeping bags made by leading manufacturers that weigh around 450-700 grams (16-27 oz) and which have the specs I want. I find only a small difference in weight compared to the quilts. However, all light sleeping gear has one notable disadvantage: they are expensive.

In spite of this, my recommendation for everyone who wants to carry a light load and plans to spend time hiking for a number of years is to cough up the dough needed for a quilt or a sleeping bag of this light weight quality. It will last most hikers at least 10-15 years if it is used 2-3 weeks per year, and will not lose much of its insulating properties during this time. This is the big difference between down and the synthetic insulation that so far has been developed.

Synthetic quilts and sleeping bags are heavier and cheaper, but my experience is that they lose considerable loft, in only a year or two, and therefore will not keep me as warm. Thanks to their price they do have a market and there are some really light quilts and a few sleeping bags with synthetic insulation that will keep you warm in temperatures around freezing without weighing more than 900-1,000 grams (2 lbs). But most of the ones that handle these temperatures are huge and voluminous lumps that weigh 1.5-2 kilos (3-4 lbs). This means that they can increase the pack weight with a kilo (2 lbs) or more, for the same function as the light down bags. I would think more than twice before buying one of those. Again, I might add that I have three-four of them in my basement and a total of 13-14 sleeping bags collected during four decades by a guy that does not believe in throwing things away.

The experienced hiker will no doubt have an easier job motivating the investment of a really light sleeping bag. The less experienced might hesitate because of the cost. My advice is to think twice and avoid buying something semi-expensive and semi-good that will leave you semi-satisfied. You might try to borrow or rent a really light bag if possible. Even for kids, these bags are a good investment, as they can use them for 10-15 years or longer. And you have in fact saved a lot of money on all your other light weight gear, as most of it is far less expensive than the heavy stuff. At least, the three big ones are. If you want to save peanuts in weight by getting a titanium whatchamacallit instead of a regular one, you can expect to pay a lot and save only very little weight.

Sleeping pad

For photos and updates, see
the live part of this book at
www.smarterbackpacking.com

*Pads for resting and sleeping can be really heavy,
but if you separate insulation from padding you can
sleep both soft and warm.*

Pads have one main function: to insulate your body
from the cold ground while you are sitting or lying down.
Personally, I need an extra function in order to sleep
well; a soft pad.

It is important to be aware that the comfort of resting
softly often will come at the price of a considerable
weight. If you want a well-padded and comfortable
sleeping pad based on self-inflating foam, synthetic
insulation or even down, the larger models often weigh
more than one kilo (2 lbs 3 oz). If you chose a minimal,
closed-cell pad which insulates but provides less comfort,
the pad will weigh around 100 grams (3 oz).

I prefer something in between, as resting on
something soft is important for my sleep and
recuperation. The best solution I have found so far is a
combination of pads. I usually carry a full-length, 180 cm

(6 feet) but thin and light closed-cell foam together with something softer and thicker for where I need softness, which is under my shoulder and hipbone, as I sleep on the side. A closed-cell foam of this length, and 5 mm (1/5 inch) thick, does not have to weigh more than 125-150 grams (5-6 oz). A short, inflatable pad, reaching from shoulder to thigh, weighs less than 300 grams (11 oz).

A type of recently introduced revolutionary air-mattresses do not only give excellent comfort and are very light, but also insulate much, much better than traditional air mattresses. Because most people do not need much softness under their legs while sleeping, my recommendation is that you pick a mattress that is maximum 120 cm (4 feet) long and leave your feet sticking out onto the closed-cell foam pad underneath the inflatable mattress.

Most of the time I carry my closed-cell pad on the outside of my pack, although there are packs with special pockets, where the folded pad fits as a sort of frame. Both solutions are excellent as I want fast and simple access to my pad at every break. I use a pair of light, elastic bungee cords to hold the rolled-up pad in place, as they are lighter than the straps that are most common. The bungee cords do not need untying; you just roll up the pad and push it through the loops you have tied.

I use this pad at almost all breaks, except really short ones, in particularly benevolent (or nasty) weather. I try to find a rock or a tree to lean against and make sure that the pad supports and insulates me from wet and cold surfaces all the way from shoulders to heels.

The padded comfort pad travels all day well protected inside my pack, as I do not need this softness until at night.

It is important that I get a good night's rest in order to be able to enjoy a hike. For some, all this takes is a torso length of closed-cell foam; for others it takes more padding. It is good to know that a hiker can achieve an extremely high level of comfort without choosing the heaviest pads on the market. Most of us do not need to rest our feet on a particularly soft pad. If you recognize this, you can save half a kilo or even a whole kilo (1-2 lbs) by using the lightest versions of soft pads in combination with insulating but thin closed-cell foam pads. This saves lots of weight at no discernible loss of comfort.

Socks

For photos and updates, see
the live part of this book at
www.smarterbackpacking.com

A strategy that works well for me, and is more or less independent of footwear, is to have three pairs of socks; wet, dry and warm. Socks can be thick or thin but unless you had planned to bring new, thick socks for every day of the week there is not that much weight to save.

The socks you choose and the weight that can be saved depends a bit on what kind of footwear you use. The kind of shoes I prefer and how I use them is described in the chapter Footwear. To summarize briefly, I use light shoes of the trail runner or water sports type and count on my feet being more or less damp most of the time. If my feet get cold I use waterproof socks, which is a fourth type of socks that I bring and they have their own chapter.

The three socks I wear (except the waterproof ones) are wet socks, warm socks and dry socks.

The wet socks are the ones that I hike in every day. They are normally a pair of really thin and light ankle socks made of nylon. Most people would consider them ladies' socks and they can be found in supermarkets or where women buy stockings. I pick the thickest I can find, which is usually 50-60 denier. They weigh around 15-20 grams (1/2-3/4 oz).

These nylon socks generally only last a week or so. It depends on the make and quality and on the terrain. I do not mind if there is a hole or even five holes in them. I twist them around on my foot (they are tube socks with no discernible heel part) to avoid holes on parts of my foot where there is wear and tear, to avoid blisters.

These very non-macho socks provide some warmth but their main function is to protect my feet a bit and prevent blisters from the shoes. If you have hard feet and soft shoes you can probably skip the wet socks and hike barefoot in your shoes.

Many lightweight hikers, particularly in North America, seem to prefer thin woollen socks as their 'wet' socks. The major disadvantage with these is that they take longer to get dry, but this may not be a big problem in less humid mountains south of the Arctic Circle.

If my feet get cold, I put on my warm socks, and on top of these, at least while I am hiking, a pair of waterproof socks. The need for warm socks comes from the fact that the thin, wet ones do not have the thickness and insulation needed inside the waterproof ones. Besides, the wet socks are usually wet. I for one need something thicker, often really thick socks. I use an ancient pair of pile socks that are quite bulky but also quick to dry. A pair of thick woollen socks will probably work as well. My warm socks usually weigh around 100 grams (3-4 oz) in my size (45/11).

Usually, I take off both my shoes and wet socks at every long break. My feet will dry quickly if they have been wet. If I do not sit around for long, this works even in chilly weather, but if not, I don my warm socks immediately. Or, I continue hiking. After the break I take off the warm socks and don the wet ones before I hit the trail again.

The dry socks are *only* used at night, as sleeping socks. I try to keep them dry at all costs, which is fairly simple if I only use them while in my sleeping bag. When I am sleeping, I often wear the warm socks on top of the dry ones. The warm ones might be a bit damp from use during breaks or inside the waterproof socks. The warm socks will dry out over night and the thinner, dry ones, will keep moisture away from my skin, thus ensuring that my feet do not get chilled from being used as dryers.

For dry socks, both thin wool and synthetics work well. Wool is in my view the nicest material next to the skin, but not all people think so and some are allergic to wool. Wool does not dry as fast as synthetics, but there are differences between synthetics as well and as they are per definition dry socks, they should never be in need of drying. On shorter excursions from the sleeping bag, I always put the waterproof socks on top of the dry socks, unless it is totally bone dry outside.

This supply of socks, wet, warm and dry, weighs around 200 grams (7 oz). This is not much lighter than a system of socks used in conjunction with boots. The difference in weight may depend more on how many pairs of socks a hiker with boots would consider necessary for a particular hike. The method I am using aims at finding a functional combination of socks that can be used with light shoes, and which, with the help of waterproof socks, will keep my feet warm no matter how cold and wet it gets, or how much hiking I have to do in snow or through water. I have found that my method works, not only for me, but also for others using the same system.

If you do not like or, which is more common, if you do not want to try the system of 'wet feet walking' which is described in the Footwear chapter, the three socks work well with boots, too. Socks that you hike in tend to get damp or wet either from the inside or the outside, no matter what kind of boots you use. So, using one pair of socks for hiking, having one pair as warm socks when you stop and carrying another that is solely used for sleeping, makes sense. In theory, you can do without your warm socks, but you run the risk of getting your dry socks wet if you use them in wet footwear, for instance, after setting up camp.

When my feet get wet – and they most likely will after a day or two of rain, no matter what the market spiel for these particular boots says – it is it is rather meaningless to replace the wet socks with a pair of dry ones, because they will get wet too, from the wet shoes. This is an endless circle; you can have your pack full of socks and make them wet one after the other. So, I feel I might as well forget about keeping my feet dry, keep my dry socks dry and resign to the fact that the wet socks will stay wet.

You could say that I have changed an unavoidable circumstance into a strategy. In any event, for my comfort it certainly is important that I have one pair of dry socks to put on when crawling into my sleeping bag. Then I can always get warm.

Socks, waterproof

For photos and updates, see
the live part of this book at
www.smarterbackpacking.com

Waterproof socks can be used in combination with most types of footwear when you are hiking. I have found that the best combination, weight wise, is to use them with light, quick-drying trail runner type shoes. Most of the waterproof socks I have used do not last for very long, so I only use them when my feet run the risk of getting cold even while on the move. Wearing light shoes and not having to care if my feet get wet or not, gives me a freedom I really appreciate.

Waterproof socks are an important part of a system of footwear that works better than anything I have tried in the soggy and cool Scandinavian mountains. You will find more information about this system in the chapter *Shoes and socks.*

This system of shoes and socks means that your feet are damp or wet most of the time, that is, if you are moving in a maritime/coastal climate. Continental/

inland climate with really hot weather and no rain is different, but also easier on your feet. Hiking with damp feet is not as unpleasant as you may think. Many people agree with me, once they have tried it. But I understand that you may be sceptical if you have not tried it, so please bear with me while I explain the mechanics of it.

There are some good reasons to keep your feet dry; feet become cold more easily when they are wet than when they are dry. But I found that this seldom happens as long as you are on the move, although I am a person whose feet easily get chilled.

When I notice that my feet are beginning to chill and I realize that whatever chills them does not seem to have any end in sight (walking on snowfields usually has a visible end, while cold rain pouring down hour after hour does not), then I don my waterproof socks. I have used Sealskinz and Rocky Goretex with good results. Goretex and Mextex also make different kinds of socks for bicycling. Some friends of mine told me they are pleased with these kinds of socks. The socks usually weigh 100-150 grams (3-5 oz) a pair.

All waterproof socks I have used so far unfortunately have a very short lifespan. This will probably change with time as materials improve. But at this point I do not count on them lasting more than around 200 kilometers (15 miles) or one week. This is why I try to use them as sparingly as possible.

In the chapter called *Socks* I describe how I combine the waterproof socks with other socks in a functional way. Waterproof socks can of course be used in combination with almost any footwear, as most tend to leak sooner or later. However, combining waterproof socks with heavy boots makes your feet heavy. You get the most bang for your buck if you act according to "the principle of the wet foot" and use very light and quick-drying shoes.

As for light and quick-drying shoes, my current favorites are mesh water sport shoes. Getting your feet wet in a pair of padded Mextex boots is a completely different and much more uncomfortable experience. This wrinkles your skin and softens your feet, making them susceptible to blisters.

If you look at the history of mankind, from when people lived in caves and onwards, we have been able to keep our feet dry in all weathers only during a very brief period of time. A majority of human beings living on our planet do not have this opportunity even today. If it is wet outside, your feet simply will get wet.

Trying to make a summary of my ramblings this means that my main advice for you in this chapter is:

a) Wet feet are not necessarily a threat to comfort or survival

b) Wet feet do not necessarily become cold feet

Most of you hikers have experienced wet feet no matter what shoes you are wearing and know that your feet stay reasonably warm as long as you keep moving. The water in the shoes and socks is warmed by your skin, like when you are using a neoprene wetsuit. This helps keep you warm as long as the warm water is not replaced by cold water too frequently.

The technique for shoes and socks that I have used successfully for a number of years and a number of hikes, some for more than 500 kilometers (350 miles) hikes on Scandinavian mountain tundra, is based on well drained, quick-drying shoes and socks.

You may not feel comfortable when you for the first time of the day have to put your sleeping bag-warmed feet into a glacial stream. But once you accept that this is part of the deal, your life has changed. You are free.

You are now free to stop tethering on tussocks, balancing on rocks and tramping on boughs to keep the dangerous water from pouring over the rim of your boots; free to skip taking care of and greasing your boots as carefully as you are pampering a newborn child; free to not incessantly change more or less damp socks for dry ones – socks that also become damp, and so on, until there are no more dry socks in your pack.

You are free to not take off boots and socks, tie them to your pack, put on your camp shoes, ford three meters (10 feet), put on your boots and socks, hike 100 meters (300 feet), take off your boots and socks, tie them to your pack, put on your camp shoes, ford 5 meters (15 feet) and so on ad nauseam…

The foot free walker just walks. A creek does not make him break his stride; he just wades through with pants and shoes. Thin and quick-drying pants and shoes bring back warmth and have shed most of the water after 50 meters (150 feet).

I look at the waterproof socks as the shells of my feet. Their weight in combination with light shoes should be compared to so-called waterproof boots. You will save hundreds of grams, maybe even kilos (tens of ounces to several pounds) by using waterproof socks in combination with light shoes. You can then save maybe 30-60 grams (1-2 oz) by choosing different types of waterproof socks.

Stuff sacks

For photos and updates, see
the live part of this book at
www.smarterbackpacking.com

A back pack is not waterproof. Therefore, you need an absolutely waterproof storage for your sleeping bag. A similar (or the same) stuff sack for extra clothing is also recommended. Bags of this kind are available and do not weigh much, but they must be completely waterproof. The rest of the gear in your pack can either stand getting wet or can be packed in smaller plastic bags. Sometimes a small mesh bag can be useful for managing some small pieces of gear.

Stuff sacks have several functions. To me, the paramount function is to keep vital pieces of equipment dry in all conditions. Vital gear to me is the sleeping bag/quilt and extra clothing. Another function of stuff sacks is keeping things organized in the pack. This could readily be overdone with lots and lots of bags and sacks.

Some systems of stuff sacks feature colour coding for different types of gear and instructions on how to pack them. If these sacks are made of sturdy fabrics and "hardwearing" zippers, these systems may weigh a lot. In my opinion, the advantages of those kinds of systems are in no way proportionate to their weight, and some of them are not even fully waterproof in all conditions.

If you are a lightweight backpacker, you have a fairly small amount of gear to begin with. This in itself is liberation – it is easy to pack up everything in the morning and get moving. To keep track of small stuff you can manage with simple systems. The best way is to use transparent bags, so you can see what you are rummaging for. Mesh bags are good for stuff that can not be damaged by water. Small mesh bags for laundry that you can find in many supermarkets are great, light and inexpensive.

For pieces of gear that should be kept in waterproof bags I use plastic Ziploc bags, also purchased at the supermarket. Some brands produce really tough bags and some do not. All you can do is try them out. There seems to be no visible difference between bags of varying quality. Normally I only use one fairly small bag of that kind, but some stuff might be stored inside this bag in a bag of its own – odds and ends like duct tape, band aids, needle-and-floss and such.

Do not expect your pack to be waterproof, not even if you use an extra rain cover. If it rains for half a day, things do get wet inside. Seams leak, and the part of your pack resting against your back is not protected by the rain cover. Hence, I never use rain covers, because they do not fulfil their primary function.

In any event, most of the stuff in the pack can handle water very well. Stove, spoon, cup, tent and food are either waterproof in themselves or packed in plastic bags (like much of the food).

What you have to keep dry at all costs is your sleeping bag. As long as you have a dry sleeping bag, a roof over your head and some food, you can always get warm. If your sleeping bag is wet, however, hypothermia could be close at hand and then your life is in danger.

Unfortunately, I have yet to find a single stuff sack sold with a sleeping bag that is truly waterproof; and by waterproof I mean resistant to immersion.

Over the years I have used numerous methods for keeping my sleeping bag dry and most of the systems have sooner or later let water in. Plastic bags are waterproof, but they are not always easy to close completely, without leakage. Even sturdy bags tend to puncture, due to sharp twigs or even fingers, unless they are very robust, and then heavy. This is also my experience of using Mylar bags for cooking turkeys.

Thin, dry bags in silnylon are available on the market. Some of them do not hold water if you turn them inside out and fill them from the tap. In my opinion, they should not show a drop of water on the outside after an hour of hanging like that in my shower.

Even the ones that hold water tend to do it for a short while only. After a period of use they tend to start leaking a bit.

So far, bags I found to be completely waterproof are somewhat sturdier dry bags or dry sacks made out of around 70 denier coated fabric. They hold the sleeping bag bone dry even if you swim with your pack (which I have done). For a light sleeping bag, a dry sack need not be larger than 10-15 liters (10-15 US quarts) and those generally weigh around 90-100 grams (3 oz). Few things of that weight in my pack feel like a better investment in security.

Not quite as important but recommended is to use a similar, smaller bag for extra clothing, like a warm jacket, sleeping socks and such. You can also put the clothes in your bigger stuff sack, but if you pack the clothes together with the sleeping bag in the bottom of your pack, it is more difficult to get out extra clothing during the day.

To be remembered is that all dry bags only are waterproof for a while. Try them out by filling them with water at home before a hike. Smaller leaks can be fixed with duct tape or a drop of silicone. But sooner or later you will have to buy a new bag. Then you can probably buy one that is as good and hardwearing as your old one, but lighter, because fabrics and waterproofing are improved all the time.

You can save 200-300 grams (6-11 oz) or more by using light and few stuff sacks.

Towel

For photos and updates, see
the live part of this book at
www.smarterbackpacking.com

*While backpacking, you can do very well without
having a towel for drying yourself after washing.
But sometimes a small piece of synthetic cloth can
be useful to wipe off condensation in your tent. If
you do not want to spend a lot of money, you buy
the cloth in the grocery store.*

Towels of any kind are not normally found in my pack
since I have found that I do not need them. However,
there are really light towels that might be worth
considering. Bringing an ordinary towel or even a bath
towel is very poor weight economy. It has several
disadvantages. Towels are usually made of cotton, which
is an inexpensive material and absorbs moisture well.
But ordinary towels rely on circumstances ensuring that
you can let them dry between uses. You have that at
home, but not out on the trail. My own experience of
bringing towels on my hikes was that the towel quickly
became a soggy lump, that was not only heavy in the

pack and made other things wet, but also was useless for its purpose because it was already wet.

Of course, there are circumstances, such as a warm and dry climate, in which a cotton towel might work, but do not bother. There are better things to bring along.

Because I manage well without a towel, I am a bit reserved towards the frightfully expensive micro-fiber towels that are sold in outdoor stores. If I should need a cloth like that, I prefer to buy the same thing (but not the same brand of course) in a grocery store or at a gas station, at a 90% discount comparatively.

Washing on the trail is mostly about hands and face. If I use my hand to wipe my face and then shake my hands, I will be dry in a minute or two. I do not really need a towel for that, as I am in no hurry. It is mostly a matter of changing a habit since childhood. This new habit is pretty easy to practice at home as well.

If I bathe or wash my hair, I will do this around noon, when it is warm and the sun is shining. Air-drying works fine then. If not, I wipe off most of the surface water on my skin with a piece of clothing, for example, my pants, and then I don my underwear which is made to handle moisture. After that I have all day to walk myself dry.

I have to admit that there is one function for which some kind of towel or cloth can be useful. That is to wipe condensation of the inside of tents and tarps. The best choice for this is a small piece of micro-fiber cloth that can be bought in grocery stores. They are light and absorb moisture well, and most important, they will dry reasonably easily, even in damp and cold weather. Pick a small size, or cut one in half, and wring it out a couple of times extra instead.

For the less experienced backpacker, the thought of a pack without a towel might seem strange, but believe me, I have not brought a towel along for many years, and I am still alive. It is a case of changing your inherent thought patterns. If you do not do that, your pack will never be one ounce lighter.

You can save 100-200 grams (3-7 oz) by skipping the towel or by picking a really small and light one.

Umbrella

For photos and updates, see
the live part of this book at
www.smarterbackpacking.com

Umbrellas are ridiculed by many backpackers, but an umbrella is a very useful tool in relation to its weight and I do not like to be without it. It is versatile an provides comfort in many ways.

One advantage with writing a book like this is that I shamelessly can spread the gospel about my own particular favourites; and the umbrella is one of mine. Though, not many hikers use an umbrella and it cannot be called an essential piece of gear. In fact, some people made serious attempts to do that, and gave it up.

The umbrella is no substitute for rain jacket and pants, at least not in the treeless areas around the Arctic Circle, where I do most of my hiking. More details about this are found in the chapters Rain and Rain jacket. You can in fact save between 100-350 grams (3-12 oz) by leaving the umbrella at home.

The reason I want to bring this extra piece of gear is that it is so much more comfortable to hike in the rain with an umbrella compared to wearing rain jacket and rain pants. Of course, you cannot hike with an umbrella when the wind is so hard that it will ruin the umbrella, which is a counter-argument you often hear. But this requires pretty strong winds, and most rain showers are not that wind-driven. And if they are, you can easily fold up your umbrella and don your regular rain gear.

Umbrellas bring comfort in different ways. One important aspect is that it is nicer to hike in your ordinary, well-ventilated clothing than to lock up most of your perspiration inside a Mextex suit. The difference is particularly noticeable if the hike is strenuous. When you are just standing around, the difference is smaller, as the perspiration then is minimal. In that kind of a situation it is still nice to not have the water dripping from your hood all the time, but instead, you are sort of sitting inside looking out at the rain. Maybe you could even take photos without soaking your camera. The umbrella also serves as protection from wind and rain for your stove, in inclement weather, or as additional wind and rain protection under your tarp or tarp tent.

The comfort of the umbrella is not only about how it feels to have it sheltering you; it is also about "off" and "on". Everyone that has hiked in rain is familiar with the dilemma: How long is this drizzle going to last? Will it turn into hard, continuous rain or will it cease within the next five minutes?

The problem is that if you wait too long to put on your rain gear, your clothing will be soaked. And even if Mextex rain gear allows small amounts of moisture to migrate, the rain gear cannot handle the amounts that need to evaporate, for drying out the wet clothing underneath.

On the other hand, you can stop when the drizzle begins. Take off your pack, dig out your rain gear, put it on and heave the pack up onto your back again. This will take a couple of minutes. After another couple of minutes the rain might cease. So, you are walking in your rain gear, but it is not raining, and you now have another dilemma.

Will it start raining again? Then you keep your rain gear on. Or, will there be no more rain? If you decide to stop, take off your jacket and pants and put them back in the pack, it might start raining again in five minutes. On the other hand, if you keep on walking in your Mextex suit, it might not rain for hours. No matter what you choose to do, you run the risk of being damp, either from not putting on your rain gear fast enough, or from not taking it off fast enough.

The umbrella will unfold quickly when the drizzle starts and fold up just as fast when the drizzle stops. It also has the added advantage of protecting the pack quite a bit. Different aspects of protection against moisture are addressed in the chapters Stuff sacks and Rain cover. The protection offered stems from the fact that most packs are in firm contact with your back. When you hike in rain with a rain jacket, the water will run down your shoulders and back, soaking the pack in the process. So when the rain stops you cannot readily take off your rain jacket, because hoisting your wet pack back on will wet your other clothes at the back – all the way down to your underwear.

This situation does not really give you much choice, except to keep your rain jacket on, although you would be more comfortable hiking in your shirt or windshirt when it is no longer raining. You are more or less forced to keep your rain jacket on until the pack is completely dry, which can take quite a while as the moisture is locked in between your back and your pack.

On the other hand, if you use an umbrella, the rain will not run down your back and the pack will remain dry. You run no risk of wetting your dry clothes after the rain; you just fold your umbrella and keep on hiking in clothing that is optimized for the temperature and your level of exertion.

In my northern hemisphere there is seldom any use for the umbrella as a parasol, but if you hike a lot in hot and sunny climates, especially in deserts, an umbrella can make quite a difference. It can mean the difference between being uncomfortably and unbearably hot, which is a greater difference than it sounds. Hiking umbrellas with a silver dome is then a good choice.

I have mostly used ordinary, cheap umbrellas with long spikes in one end and a long wooden handle at the other. The spike I saw off, and drop some silicone in to close up the resulting hole, the handle is sawed off so that only a couple of centimetres (1 inch) remains as a sort of handle hold. These umbrellas usually weigh around 330 grams (12 oz), but special hiking umbrellas are usually up to a hundred grams (3 oz) lighter, but more expensive.

So, I have now given you a spiel on behalf of my beloved umbrella and will not mention it further in this book. At least not very much. And not very often.

Undershirt

For photos and updates, see
the live part of this book at
www.smarterbackpacking.com

*The main function of the undershirt, keeping your
torso dry, makes it a very important garment. I
prefer a really thin undershirt made of merino wool.
If I need more warmth, even in winter, I just add
another garment, thin or thick, on top of the thin
undershirt next to my skin.*

By undershirt I mean the garment I wear next to my skin.
My undershirt is also my shirt. In the Clothing chapter
you will find some important information on this. I have
found that the most important function of my
undergarments is not to keep me warm by insulating,
but by transporting moisture away from my body. Their
main purpose is to keep the surface of my skin as dry as
possible.

Cotton is the material most people use for
undergarments in everyday life. Unfortunately, cotton is
extremely unsuitable for next-to-skin garments used in
physical activity outdoors in temperate climates. This is
because cotton sucks moisture into its fibers, which then

collapse and adhere to the skin. The result is that the insulating air in the fibers disappears, and also that moisture is trapped against the surface of the skin, cooling and chilling the skin.

When we are physically active outdoors we need a garment next to the body that keeps the surface of the skin dry. That is why undergarments for hiking should be made of material that is capable of moving sweat and moisture away from the skin surface. Today there are mainly two kinds of fabrics that do this very well in all kinds of weather: synthetics and wool.

Synthetics are of various kinds. They are all petroleum-based. When in use, they have very similar characteristics, even if their chemical compositions differ. Today there is a multitude of synthetic underwear that transports moisture very well. Their main disadvantage is that they in fact smell very badly from stale sweat, if they are not washed fairly often. As far as I am concerned, they need to be washed every day. This problem has been around for a long time and the solution always seemed to be just around the corner. Even if in 2010 it is still just around the corner; it will no doubt some day be solved.

Apart from their tendency to stink, synthetics work very well for sports and hiking. They also wear extremely well. If you carry out activities that enable you to wash your clothes or if you are in a climate where clothes can be washed, or just flushed in cold water, the smell does not need to be a problem. On the other hand, if you spend a week tenting without washing your clothes, the consequences can be nauseating for people nearby. Finally, you will in fact smell so bad that you will notice it yourself!

Wool is today considered by many hikers to be the most comfortable and functional material to wear next to your skin. Wool has made a comeback thanks to new technologies and the use of short-fiber merino wool. These days, people with sensitive skin are almost all rash free when using merino underwear.

Compared to cotton, wool can soak up fairly large amounts of moisture in their fibers without collapsing. This means wool garments moves moisture away from your skin but also keeps its insulating properties. Furthermore, wool can be worn for a long, long time without smelling noticeably.

I have used both synthetics and wool garments and currently I definitely prefer wool. However, no matter which material I use, I pick the thinnest available. This is because the most important property of the undershirt is to keep my skin dry, not insulate.

I have found that it works best for me if I am not tempted to use a thicker undergarment because it has better insulating properties than a thin one. The consequences seem to be poorer moisture transport. At best, there is no difference. In any event, I prefer to keep my usual, thin undergarment and add insulating layers on top. Instead of one thick undergarment I think it is better to wear two thin ones, allowing for more flexibility. Usually I wear two in wintertime.

During summer or 3-season (spring, summer, fall) I

mostly use a short-sleeved merino shirt with a collar, although T-shirts of course are an alternative. However, my choice probably stems mostly from the fact that I think the merino shirt looks smarter when I am sitting in a trail town, lying about my daredevil escapades over a beer. But if you want me to dig out some rational reasons I could claim that a collar can be turned up, providing additional warmth around your neck.

In fall and winter I use an equally thin, but long-sleeved merino shirt. If I can find one with a zip-T-neck or a hood, that is great, but if not, I pick the thinnest and use the zip-T or hood as an insulating layer on top, when needed. When sleeping, I always wear the second one next to my skin, and the day undershirt on top of that, drying out during the night. Before starting out in the morning, I put the day shirt on and the second one goes in the pack.

By now it should be clear to readers that I carry two thin merino shirts on overnight hikes. They weigh around 200 grams (6-7 oz) a piece, in Large or XLarge. Thicker underwear can weigh 100-200 grams more. Thin, synthetic shirts may weigh around 100 grams (3 oz), particularly in small sizes. I have also used really thin polyester shirts with button front and collars and with no advertised super-duper moisture transporting characteristics. These shirts can be bought for next to nothing unless they have a known logo tacked onto them. They work very well and can actually be washed and dried during a lunch break when the weather is sunny.

However, I have found that when I use a wool shirt, I

don't need to change it after the hike, but can go home by bus, train or plane without being shunned by my fellow passengers. I used to bring a clean cotton T-shirt in my pack to be used on the trip back, but nowadays I manage without that extra weight.

Warm garment

For photos and updates, see
the live part of this book at
www.smarterbackpacking.com

*A jacket is a garment for modest physical activity.
One single light garment is usually enough to keep
you warm at breaks. A light jacket filled with down
or synthetics gives ample insulation for its weight.*

The warm layer, often also called middle layer, has the
ability to insulate in accordance with its capacity to keep
air stationary in minuscule pockets. The loftier and
fluffier the jacket is, the better it insulates. The
traditional fleece jacket or pullover is a garment that
does not hold much insulating air and also weighs quite
a bit. The slightly fluffier pile often holds more air and
insulates better. But if you want a substantial level of
insulation and low weight, you have to skip both these
hard wearing, sturdy materials.

Nowadays I usually use a light down jacket that
weighs 300-400 grams (11-13 oz) or a jacket with
synthetic insulation and a hood of about the same
weight. They are both considerably warmer than fleece.

They are also windproof and because of this, they work very well as a garment to wear on the outside of the rest of my clothes, at longer breaks. A fleece jacket should usually be worn underneath a windproof garment in order to insulate optimally.

When it is raining, you have to wear your rain jacket on top of the down or synthetic jacket. When it is only cold and windy, or when I want to avoid spilling food on my insulating garment, I usually wear my windshirt on top. If this is not enough to stay warm, I crawl partly or wholly into my sleeping bag.

My trusty old pile jacket weighed almost 700 grams (25 oz). So, there is weight to be saved by choosing something lighter and also warmer. The disadvantage is that neither down, nor synthetic jackets come cheap. However, if you choose a down jacket you have a companion for many years. The synthetic insulation so far has a much more limited lifespan.

The fleece jacket is good for kids, because of its low price and limitless capacity for wear and tear. If you combine this with a light down vest intended for adults, you have extra warmth and a combination that will last until the kids are grown, simply by replacing the fleece sweater as they grow. This solution has worked great for my kids.

Water

For photos and updates, see
the live part of this book at
www.smarterbackpacking.com

First rule: Water is heavy. Do not carry it unless you have to. Second rule: If you have to, do not use heavy water bottles. Carry 30-50 grams (1-2 oz) for a 1.5 liter (1,5 US quart) bottle, not more. Water purification is not always necessary.

Let me start out by saying that I am fortunate when it comes to water. Most of my hiking is done in arctic areas where water is abundant and clean. I have never purified water in the Swedish mountains. I only carry water when I plan to walk up on a peak somewhere and know water will be scarce on the higher levels. I do not feel that I am using my own energy for the best purpose by lugging something that is found almost anywhere at almost any time in these mountains.

The situation is different when I backpack in American mountains or deserts where water sources can be scarce. Even in fairly wet mountains such as in the Pacific Northwest of the US I usually carry 0.2-0.6 liters (1-2 pints) to be able to have a good drink every hour. In drier areas you have to carry more and in deserts you may have to carry a huge amount. When you plan for your hike, you have to research the access to water.

The same holds true for water purification. In my arctic mountains I have never purified any water and I have never come down sick during the four decades I have been rambling around there. Naturally, I use a certain amount of common sense when I choose water sources. I try to avoid water that is stagnant or water that looks or smells suspiciously. Yet, I have drunk water like that on occasion without ill effects. Brownish water with the odd bug or larvae in it is nothing to worry about; it is simply a sign that the water is good. The fact that it smells differently than the chlorinated stuff coming out of our taps is not something to be afraid of either.

If you are in doubt, in most cases it is completely sufficient to bring the water to a boil. When I move through areas where there are livestock such as cattle and sheep, and where people are abundant, I usually take along a chemical water purifier. I have used filters but find them time-consuming and heavy.

This is not a book for detailed advice on water treatment practices. You will find a bit more information in the chapter Hygiene; however, if you are novice, you should consult some of the major handbooks on backpacking that cater to the area where you do most of your hiking. If you are an experienced backpacker you probably know how you should manage water in your own backwoods.

I always bring a water bottle with a volume of 1.5-2

litres (1,5-2 US quarts). Usually, the bottle stays empty but I fill it up at a water course at mealtimes and camp, in order to have water close at hand where I am sitting and cooking. Before moving on I usually pour out any remaining water. Ordinary PET pop bottles are incredibly rugged and light considering their price (they are sort of free). I have used them for years. Lately, I have taken to using a collapsible bottle that rolls up to nearly nothing in my pack. It is lighter than a pop bottle. You can pour water that is hot and practically boiling into these bottles (including PET bottles) and put the bottle in your sleeping bag if it is chilly or the bag is damp. This is a great last resort to manage through a night when you feel cold even when you are wearing every piece of clothing while in your sleeping bag. Knowing that this is always available, you never have to carry an extra thick sleeping bag 'just in case'.

To sum it up, you can save a great deal of energy by not carrying water unless it is absolutely necessary. You have fought to save grams (ounces) in your pack. Do not spoil it all by casually adding kilos (pounds) of water. You can also save quite a bit of weight by not choosing any of the heavy water containers in various colours that are taking up so much shelf space in backpacking stores. Anyone can figure out that they are part of an extremely profitable business if they are given that much space. Never choose a container that weighs more than 50-60 grams (2 oz) for a 1.5-2 litre (1.5-2 US quarts) bottle.

Windscreen cooking

For photos and updates, see the live part of this book at **www.smarterbackpacking.com**

A windscreen increases fuel efficiency for all types of burners quite a bit. Most important is to protect the flame and lower part of the pot. That is where most of the energy transfer from flame to pot content takes place. The handy person can easily fix something from aluminium foil that does a good job. Information on different constructions abound on the Internet.

As can be seen in the Cooking chapter, there are diverse ways of heating your food. A factor to consider is that the efficiency of the flame is severely impaired when wind is hitting it and the pot. Maybe this is not a big deal if you use wood and supply of wood is abundant, but it becomes important if you carry your fuel.

In northern Europe you can buy an alcohol stove with windscreen and a set of pots that for half a century has been synonymous with the classic Trangia 25. It is a simple and practical tool that lasts forever. The Trangia is however not light, even if lighter materials have been introduced.

The Trangia windscreen and pot rest in my classic old aluminium version weighs 400 grams. This can be replaced by something made from aluminium foil that weighs less than 20-30 grams (1 oz). You need to protect the flame and the lower part of the pot. This can in fact be done to some extent by utilizing natural windscreens like rocks or small cavities, or by rigging up a sleeping pad or a backpack or other gear. But I feel it is simpler to take along a light windscreen, because it enables me to choose where I eat more from the view than from what serves as a windscreen for my stove.

Details of many more or less brilliant foil constructions can be found on the Internet. What you need is something that is simple, functional and sturdy enough. In the past, I have made windscreens that literally fell into small pieces after two days on a one week trip.

Whether you use a canister stove, an alcohol burner or some type of tablets, a simple cylinder of foil or thin tin, that surrounds the stove and pot completely, is usually the best. For several years I have used a cylinder made from titanium foil that works very well and also wears really well. This windscreen also crackles terribly when I roll it up and put it in my pack. The weight is 26 grams (1 oz).

Well worth considering is that the windscreen must not be so efficient that the flame becomes oxygen-starved. Usually air can enter around the bottom of a screen like the one I have described, if the ground is a bit uneven. Otherwise, a good idea is to punch holes at the lower end.

If you use this type of a windscreen with canister stoves you have to check that the canister does not get overheated. If the canister becomes very hot it can explode. Being warm to the touch is okay for a canister; being hot to the touch is not. Sometimes, a sort of collar, made of aluminium foil, that is positioned between the canister and the flame can keep the flame from heating the canister. This is usually not a problem in cool climates but definitely worth watching in really hot weather. In such conditions it is better to choose a windscreen that lets the air move freely around the canister and only shields the flame and the lower part of the pot.

A windscreen should not weigh more than 50-60 grams (2 oz). Lots of lighter alternatives are around, but some of them have rather short lifespan.

Windshirt

For photos and updates, see
the live part of this book at
www.smarterbackpacking.com

*A windshirt of thin, windproof but not waterproof
fabric is one of my most beloved garments. I am not
alone in having this infatuation – the windshirt is
an important part of many light packers' wardrobe.
The windshirt is much more comfortable to hike in
than a traditional shell jacket, as long as it is not
raining.*

A windshirt is a thin and light garment that is supposed
to be what the name implies; windproof. A thin
windbreaker like that on top of your undershirt/base-
layer is often enough to keep you warm while hiking,
even in chilly conditions.

I have found that even in temperatures close to
freezing, the combination of undershirt and windshirt
works very well. If the weather feels too chilly, I can put
on an extra undershirt (my night shirt) that I always
bring with me. In winter and even with temperatures
below freezing, and a biting wind, this combination is
usually enough to keep me warm as long as I am on the

move.

At breaks I usually put on an insulated garment on my torso, and if it starts raining I use my umbrella. If this is not enough, say, in hard wind and rain, I don my rain jacket.

Some windshirts do not weigh more than 50-80 grams (2-3 oz). I have in fact seen windshirts lighter than that. They have only a chest part and let the pack protect the back.

Personally, I prefer a slightly heavier windshirt that weighs 100-150 grams (4-5 oz) in my size. The reason is, I really believe that the hood that comes with these heavier garments is worth its weight. You will find few hoods on windshirts that weigh less than 100 grams (3 oz). But fabrics are becoming lighter and I am sure windshirts with hoods that weigh below 100 grams (3 oz) will soon be available.

Many people consider the windshirt unnecessary because their rain jacket is windproof. But I definitely belong to the group of people who do not want to wear a rain jacket unless it is raining. They are all right for standing around in the rain, but not for consistent hiking. At home, when waiting for the bus, I like using different kinds of Mextex garments, but while hiking, I find the condensation inside a bother, and I prefer to not use my rain jacket unless there is a considerable amount of rain and wind. More details about this are found in the chapters on Rain and Rain jackets.

I avoid windshirts that are made of fabrics that ventilate poorly. Be aware that some windshirts are almost as waterproof as rain gear. They can be useful if you are using a poncho or a cape both as rain gear and shelter for the night. If it is raining when you are setting up or breaking camp, a water-resistant windshirt can be valuable while you are neither under the roof or inside the poncho. But for all other occasions I prefer a windshirt that breathes well and has a minimal DWR (durable water repellent) coating.

A windshirt is made of very tightly woven fabrics that are impregnable to biting insects. This makes the windshirt a very useful garment during bug season as it is also thin and cool.

Looking at weight, a thin windshirt and a light rain jacket often weigh less than most waterproof shell jackets you find in the stores. So my conclusion is: wear your windshirt, and wear on it when it is not raining. That way your rain jacket will see less wear when it is not raining and will be water-proof when it needs to be, even if you choose a very light and thin rain jacket.

The windshirt is very much underrated by most people that are not using it, but a great favorite among its followers. It is light, inexpensive, and makes it possible for you to have a light and cheap rain jacket that still does the job when needed.

About the author

Jorgen Johansson was a traditional backpacker for decades until he started using and adapting ultralight and lightweight backpacking techniques to the demanding circumstances of the tundra mountains of northern Europe.

He has hiked in many areas of the northern hemisphere, including the Alps, Ireland, Canada, Alaska and other parts of the US.

He has published several books on backpacking in Swedish and has a popular blog. Apart from his books he also contributes articles to outdoor magazines and holds courses and lectures on lightweight hiking techniques. He lives just north of Stockholm, Sweden.

More info can be found at *www.smarterbackpacking.com*